3

# Multitasking in the Digital Age

# Synthesis Lectures on Human-Centered Informatics

Editor

**John M. Carroll**, *Penn State University*

Human-Centered Informatics (HCI) is the intersection of the cultural, the social, the cognitive, and the aesthetic with computing and information technology. It encompasses a huge range of issues, theories, technologies, designs, tools, environments, and human experiences in knowledge work, recreation and leisure activity, teaching and learning, and the potpourri of everyday life. The series publishes state-of-the-art syntheses, case studies, and tutorials in key areas. It shares the focus of leading international conferences in HCI.

Multitasking in the Digital Age
Gloria Mark

www.morganclaypool.com

ISBN: 9781627057493 print
ISBN: 9781627057509 ebook

DOI 10.2200/S00635ED1V01Y201503HCI029

A Publication in the Morgan and Claypool Publishers series
*SYNTHESIS LECTURES ON HUMAN-CENTERED INFORMATICS #29*
Series Editor: John M. Carroll, Penn State University

Series ISSN 1946-7680 Print 1946-7699 Electronic

# Multitasking in the Digital Age

**Gloria Mark**
University of California, Irvine

*SYNTHESIS LECTURES ON HUMAN–CENTERED INFORMATICS #29*

# ABSTRACT

In our digital age we can communicate, access, create, and share an abundance of information effortlessly, rapidly, and nearly ubiquitously. The consequence of having so many choices is that they compete for our attention: we continually switch our attention between different types of information while doing different types of tasks—in other words, we multitask. The activity of information workers in particular is characterized by the continual switching of attention throughout the day. In this book, empirical work is presented, based on ethnographic and sensor data collection, which reveals how multitasking affects information workers' activities, mood, and stress in real work environments.

Multitasking is discussed from various perspectives: activity switching, interruptions as triggers for activity switching, email as a major source of interruptions, and the converse of distractions: focused attention. All of these factors are components of information work. This book begins by defining multitasking and describing different research approaches used in studying multitasking. It then describes how multiple factors occur to encourage multitasking in the digitally-enabled workplace: the abundance and ease of accessing information, the number of different working spheres, the workplace environment, attentional state, habit, and social norms. Empirical work is presented describing the nature of multitasking, the relationship of different types of interruptions and email with overload and stress, and patterns of attention focus. The final chapter ties these factors together and discusses challenges that information workers in our digital age face.

## KEYWORDS

multitasking, interruptions, attention focus, email, information work, sensors, in situ study

# Contents

# Acknowledgments

This book is dedicated to Alfred who keeps me focused, to Michaela and Natalie who keep me open to new possibilities, and to Lilli, my mother, who always inspires me to be positive.

# CHAPTER 1

# Introduction

We are living in the digital age. Never before in history could we communicate with others, and access, create, and share so much information so effortlessly, rapidly, and nearly ubiquitously. When we turn to our computers or smart phones we are constantly tempted by innumerable choices of information to consume and produce. The consequence of having so many choices is that they compete for our attention. When we use digital media we continually switch our attention between different types of information while doing different types of tasks—in other words, we multitask.

In her book *A Prehistory of Ordinary People*, Monica Smith (2010) claims that multitasking has been around for a long time—over 1.5 million years in fact, since our bipedal ancestors began to build tools. To survive, they had to continually monitor their environment. Hunters and gatherers would forage for food while at the same time searching for resources to make tools, looking out for their children and of course keeping an eye out for predators. Their ability to survive depended on their skill at multitasking. With over one million years of experience, one might expect that by now we would have nailed this multitasking skill.

But as I will discuss in this book, it is not the case. There are consequences of having interfaces that enable us to access and contribute so much information so readily. One consequence is that people can be overloaded and overburdened when switching attention among a variety of information. People are overloaded not only due to processing the sheer volume of information but also through continually reorienting to new information as they switch. The concern about information overload is not new. With the development of every new media an alarm has sounded about the danger brought upon us by too much information. The fear of not being able to remember the knowledge being produced was recorded as far back as the 13th century:

> *"Since the multitude of books, the shortness of time and the slipperiness of memory do not allow all things which are written to be equally retained in the mind...."* (Vincent of Beuvais, preface to Speculum Maius, 1255, in Blair, 2003).

With the printing press, came fears that the multitude of books produced would affect people's health, leading to melancholy, expressed in this quote from Robert Burton who wrote *The Anatomy of Melancholy* in 1621:

> *"As already, we shall have a vast Chaos and confusion of books, we are oppressed with them, dour eyes ache with reading, our fingers with turning"* (Burton, 1621, pg. 38).

These two quotes appeared before people had the capacity to switch almost effortlessly among different sources and types of information. What is new about information overload in our current digital age is that the factors contributing to overload have changed. First, not only can we access an abundance of stored and streaming information but also we can produce information rapidly with low effort. The barriers of accessing information have nearly disappeared as soon as one turns on their laptop or smartphone. But there is also a second-order effect of such access to information: we can switch rapidly among different information sources and activities, and our attention is continually refocusing. This constant shifting and refocusing of attention has led to a new way to conceptualize information overload in our digital age.

Thus, with the development of every new form of information technology came apprehension of an onslaught of information. Returning to the present, several years ago a report on information usage described that Americans consume outside of the workplace, on average, over 100,000 words a day (Bohn and Short, 2009). People consume this information through digital devices, communication networks, television, and print media. This statistic is based on a range of Americans: teachers, plumbers, stockbrokers, retailers, manufacturing line workers, housewives, and so on. Surprisingly, this statistic reports on information consumed outside of the workplace. What about information consumed and managed in the workplace by professionals who deal with digital information on a daily basis?

A large segment of our population works in professions where dealing with digital information in some form is central to their work. These people are information workers whose jobs are primarily concerned with managing information. I use the term "information worker" as opposed to knowledge worker—people who create value by applying their knowledge—as the former is a more generic term that can apply across a range of professions. Information workers spend much, if not most, of their day dealing with digital information. Information workers can create, exchange, modify, combine, and respond to information as part of their day-to-day work experience. They use laptops, smart phones, and a range of applications: email, productivity apps, social media, communication media, calendars, and scheduling systems, as they process information. The information workers of our current digital age deal with an amount of information that is many orders of magnitude greater than literate people did a century ago, or even 50 years prior.

Information work is performed by people in a variety of work roles in numerous fields, for example, administrators, managers, financial analysts, consultants, programmers, lawyers, journalists, professors, accountants, and many, many more. To give a very broad estimate of the wide range of people in the U.S. who do information work, eight occupation categories of the U.S. Department of Labor would likely have most workers in these categories doing information work (example categories are business and financial services operations, architecture and engineering operations, office and administrative service operations). However, more and more, other occupations (e.g., production operations) involve managing information on computers to a large degree. Information work is widespread, and so is the consequent work on multiple activities and switching between these activities.

Thus, information workers deal with large amounts of information on a daily basis. However, simply providing a descriptive account of the average daily amount of information consumed and exchanged as it passes among information workers does not provide a clear picture of the human experience in dealing with it. To provide a view into how the digital age affects our lives I look at the digital experience from a behavioral perspective. The main question that I address in this book is: How does working with digital information on a daily basis affect information workers in the workplace? I focus on the practice of multitasking, which includes the effects of interruptions and how attention is directed to various activities.

This book explores multitasking for information workers in the 21st century. In the field of HCI, there has been a vast amount of research devoted to understanding the experience of people using single applications. We are only recently starting to address the idea that single applications are used in a wider context of other applications and devices. In this book I argue that it is important to expand the lens of studying information use to the entire *ecology* of digital media use, especially when considering it in a real-world context. There are several points I will emphasize in information work.

- Information technology use occurs in a context. It is therefore important to study technology usage in the context in which it occurs.

- People work on multiple projects using different applications and devices.

- People are constantly exposed to a wealth of stored as well as incoming information, which poses a challenge to manage.

This book explores the consequences for information workers of working on multiple projects and having easy access to so much digital information. While the sheer abundance of information raises a number of fascinating questions (Is it making us smarter? Have we become more articulate? Are we more productive? Are we more efficient? How overwhelmed are we with information?), I would like to focus on one issue in particular—how this plethora of information affects our ability to focus and concentrate on the task at-hand.

The ability to focus in this information environment is a critical question. Marshall McLuhan described that we become what we behold (McLuhan, 1994). As the Internet is digital, nonlinear, and discrete, our attention has come to mirror this; our attention is easily fragmented. Ironically, the improvisatory nature of the growth of the Internet has given rise to the improvisatory behavior of its users. As Mcluhan also describes: *"Technology leads to new structures of feeling and thought."* McLuhan described that the development of the print medium led people to arrange their perceptions to conform to the printed page. In the digital era, people similarly are arranging their perceptions to conform to the stimuli afforded by digital media.

More and more organizations are realizing that the challenge in focusing attention is pervasive in information work. A 2013 study of 12,115 employees (94% in white collar jobs) revealed that 66% felt that they could not focus on one thing at a time (Schwartz and Porath, 2014). In this digital age, we are faced with new challenges in focusing our attention, given the ease and seductiveness to retrieve information. Using digital media requires developing new skills in focusing attention in light of the distractions available online as well as off line. When we problematize the notion of attention focus as a consequence of the digital age, it raises a number of related questions such as how focus (or lack thereof) affects our levels of stress, our communication with others, our ability to reinstate work when interrupted, and so on. I will address these topics by discussing the everyday experience of information workers in managing their digital information.

Multitasking is a multi-faceted topic. In this book I will cover different topics related to multitasking. In Chapter 2, I provide a definition of multitasking and describe different research approaches used in studying multitasking. Chapter 3 discusses factors that can contribute to explaining why people multitask so extensively in information work. Chapter 4 delves into empirical work explaining the nature of multitasking among information workers. A major impetus that triggers multitasking behavior is interruptions. Chapter 5 describes studies of interruptions and explores the relationship of different types of interruptions and multitasking behavior. A main source of interruptions is email—either through notifications or self-checking. Chapter 6 focuses on email and how it not only affects multitasking but how it affects stress and mood in the workplace. Chapter 7 addresses the converse of distractions and activity switching: attention focus. This chapter reviews types of focused attention and discusses factors that affect people's focus in the workplace. Chapter 8 ties these factors together and discusses challenges that information workers in our digital age face.

CHAPTER 2

# What is Multitasking?

What exactly is meant by multitasking? Different disciplines have approached the subject of multitasking ranging from cognitive science, psychology, education, human factors, to management science. A wealth of laboratory studies exist which have examined people's ability to conduct two tasks simultaneously, varying along domains, task complexity, task duration, and other measures. Yet only fairly recently in the last ten years have researchers become interested in multitasking when doing computer work. Here I examine multitasking in a real-world environment as opposed to a controlled setting in a laboratory.

Different fields have developed different notions of multitasking. In the field of communications, media multitasking refers to the use of two or more media at the same time, for example, when people work on the computer while listening to music. Media multitasking is not a new phenomenon; people have long used multiple media at the same time such as listening to the radio or television while reading. The use of multiple media in synchronous use has been studied extensively with young people. Comparing the use of different media across ages, young people were found to use more different media at the same time as opposed to an older generation, such as listening to music while reading (Carrier et al., 2009). However, with the advent of the Internet, an additional source of media is available to combine with other media. People can listen to music online while reading—however, this combination of media existed since the radio was invented. With Internet use, college-aged students were found to use more multiple media compared to when doing academic reading, leisure reading, or when watching television (Mokhtari et al., 2009). Most college students reported using instant messaging when doing schoolwork, as well as when doing computer and non-computer activities (Golder et al., 2007).

The field of psychology has considered the performance of multiple concurrent tasks in everyday life such as walking and humming a song or driving while talking. Here, the performance of primary and secondary task performance, also known as dual task performance, has been studied extensively in the laboratory, with tasks such as reading while keeping digits in memory (for a review, see Pashler, 1994). This notion of multitasking refers to performing multiple concurrent tasks (cf. Salvucci and Taatgen, 2008).

In this book I examine multitasking in terms of people working on multiple tasks using digital media. In this context, switching among tasks generally occurs on the same device—the computer where the information is stored. While listening to online music, for example through a program like Spotify, combined with writing a document can be considered multitasking, another form of multitasking is switching between different pieces of information, which may be all contained on the computer. Switching activities can also occur among the computer and use of other devices, materials, or in-person interactions.

When considering work on multiple tasks from this standpoint, the definition of multitasking that I use is based on the idea of time-sharing in computers. Time-sharing refers to the sharing of computer resources among multiple users based on an algorithmic design. In contrast to the earlier batch processing, where single programs were run in succession, the idea behind time-sharing was that the computer could more efficiently distribute resources among multiple users. The computer had a central processing unit that switched almost synchronously among different users.

The analogy of time-sharing of computer resources can apply to describe how humans multitask. By multitasking, I refer to the interleaving of different activities. In contrast to the idea of working on multiple concurrent tasks such as listening to music and reading, when tasks are interleaved, attention is switching back and forth between different tasks. This can occur quite rapidly, especially when task switching on the computer interface. Some accounts of multitasking explain that the simultaneous performance of tasks can occur, but it is dependent on a number of factors, such as if they use different modalities such as audio and visual input (Wickens, 2008). These accounts generally hold when one of the tasks can be performed automatically, such as driving a car while talking.

Multitasking, with regards to computer work among information workers, can be viewed at different levels of granularity. At a very high level, we can talk about switching between different projects. Projects could be an academic paper, the development of a software tool, or a law case. A lawyer might be responsible for several law cases and the work on these different projects could be interleaved. As academics, we are responsible for conducting different research projects, writing grants, teaching classes, mentoring students, doing committee work, performing service to the university, and service to the external community such as reviewing papers or organizing a conference. In a typical day, one would switch constantly between these different projects.

Projects, in turn, can be further broken down into subprojects. We can also focus a lens on multitasking as switching between subtasks, such as switching between different chapters of a larger book project. In writing an academic paper, one needs to do a literature review, design and conduct a study, analyze data, and then write up the results. Unfortunately, these subtasks are not always done in an order to optimize efficiency. One might switch between the literature review and analyzing the data, and then switch to writing the introduction of the paper. These are all switches within the same larger project: the academic paper. But imagine now that one is also working on a second paper. One might then switch from the literature review of the first paper to data analysis of the second. But academics in general do not only just write papers. They mentor students, serve on committees, review papers, write letters of recommendations, sit on task forces, organize conferences—the list goes on and on. So, although we may have good intentions of starting one project and finishing it through to completion, life intervenes, so to speak.

Multitasking can even be viewed at an even finer level of granularity, in terms of more "micro" operations such as switching between a Word document and phone call. In other words, the different activities can be viewed with a more magnified lens that provides more detail. When studying multitasking in a real-world environment, it is useful to be able to focus on activities at different levels of granularity.

When multitasking occurs in a real-world environment with digital media use such as in the workplace or home, it is not only the switching between different projects, but also switching between computer activity and offline activity. Thus, one can switch between a computer game and interaction with a person, or writing on a Word doc and phone call. Importantly, as one switches activities, consequently so does one's attention. When one switches, one needs to reorient to a new set of information. Thus, when switching between activities, regardless of the level of granularity that the observer is concerned with, attention shifts as well. Thus, multitasking is inherently tied to the ability to focus. The faster one switches between activities and information, the shorter is one's duration of focus on any information source. Switching fast can also induce stress. As we have limited attentional resources, we are straining these resources as we switch our attention.

Understanding multitasking involves a consideration of temporal patterns of activity, as tasks are interleaved over time. The organization of time can vary across cultures, as Hall and Hall (1990) observed, which suggests that multitasking behavior might also vary across cultures. If we consider organizational culture in particular, we might expect there to be different cultures of temporal patterns for how work is managed. Organizations that place a higher value on schedules and punctuality have cultures that tend to be more monochronic, a style of work where employees work on one task at a time, preferably through to completion, before moving on to another task (Bluedorn et al., 1999). Polychronicity, on the other hand, refers to working on a number of different activities at the same time. The ability to do polychronic work is an advantage in some professions such as with air traffic controllers who must monitor different simultaneous aircraft trajectories.

As a cultural variable, polychronicity involves values and beliefs. Bluedorn et al. (1992) proposed that individuals have preferences for monochronic or polychronic activity. Interestingly, Bluedorn et al. (1999) described that people who do monochronic work would view unexpected events such as phone calls or face-to-face interactions as disruptions to their work. People who are true polychronics would view such unexpected events as part of their polychronic work environment. In fact, polychronicity has advantages in giving people an overview of all their projects. Monochronic work can lead people to lose a larger perspective on other tasks. Perhaps from an evolutionary perspective, it was an advantage to be polychronic. One needed to keep an eye out for bears or snakes while foraging for food.

Most people, however, tend to prefer monochronic work—switching activities and rapidly changing the focus of attention goes against most people's nature (Bluedorn et al., 1999). But in the age of computing and the Internet, polychronic work has become commonplace. People have become polychronic to react to the demands of the workplace, and in fact, data shows that work-place demands significantly predict multitasking (König et al., 2010). Answering emails, Instant messaging, texting, searching on the Internet for information, or using Facebook all contribute to polychronicity as they involve attention switching between a main task and these activities, which may or may not supplement the main task. Polychronicity is correlated with the personality trait of striving for achievement (and also impatience), but not with performance, although this may depend on the particular work context (Conte et al., 1999).

The internal mechanism that governs multitasking is not clear and different psychological perspectives have been proposed to explain the process of multitasking. I review here some key theories. One theory is that working memory supports people in task-switching as people need to keep some amount of information available concerning their different tasks. Switching attention between different activities involves different processes: storing, transforming, connecting, activating, and modifying information. These processes are proposed to be handled by working memory (Oberaurer et al., 2000). The working memory component of coordination is proposed to predict the speed of multitasking whereas the storage component of working memory is proposed to predict multitasking errors (Buehner et al., 2006). These results were based on various monitoring and recall tasks in a laboratory setting.

Some accounts explain multitasking by the allocation of attentional resources. In Kahneman's (1973) theory of attention, there is a single general pool of resources that are allocated among different tasks. Attentional resources are limited, and are selectively allocated to processing different activities. Performance degrades when the limited capacity is exceeded. Other accounts assume multiple cognitive resources. Navon and Gopher (1979) proposed that distinct resources combine to perform tasks. If tasks utilize different resources then they can be performed simultaneously with no performance degradation. If, however, they require the same resources, then it is assumed that resources are flexibly allocated. However, performance degrades as more simultaneous tasks are performed. A multiple resource model of multitasking is presented by Wickens (2008) that explains three dimensions: stages of processing (selection of tasks is processed differently than the performance of tasks which uses cognitive resources), codes of processing (e.g., spatial activity uses different codes than linguistic activity), and modalities (e.g., audio stimuli uses different processing resources than visual stimuli). The theory explains that multitasking performance will increase as tasks involve different levels of these dimensions.

From a task perspective, Norman and Shallice (1986) considered that every activity or task that people perform utilizes a particular set of cognitive resources. Typing on a Word document, or posting on Facebook, or engaging in an interaction, use different mental resources. Norman and Shallice view these as "active schemas," i.e., the schema of typing on a Word document is activated when a particular set of conditions occur. Actions can be routine, such as when one reaches for the telephone upon ringing, or they can be deliberate as when one opens a Word document to begin working on a book chapter. Checking email when a notification occurs may well be a routine action.

Another perspective is that of balancing internal control and external demands. Monsell (2003) described that every action we do is related to a negotiation of internal goals and external influences. Monsell further described that one's ability to perform a task involves a balance of endogenous control to protect one from distraction of irrelevant stimuli, yet still enabled one to retain flexibility to respond to important events. There is a cost to switching tasks: task responses in laboratory trials take longer after a switch as opposed to repeating the same task. When people switch tasks, they need to reconfigure their schemas (per Norman and Shallice), in what Monsell described as "mental gear-changing." The switch cost can be thought of as the time that it takes to reconfigure the schema.

More recent accounts of multitasking use computational models to explain data. Kieras et al. (2000) proposed a computational model of multitasking behavior, EPIC, which explains that an executive mental process controls task switching behavior. Performance decrements are explained by the strategies used to manage different tasks. An alternative account to the use of an executive control is that of threaded cognition (Salvucci and Taatgen, 2008). Here it is proposed that people can maintain multiple goals that result in independent processing threads that alternate in acquiring and managing resources.

The different definitions and accounts of multitasking all attest to the commonplace occurrence of multitasking in ordinary life. Multitasking is a way of life; most people are involved in multiple projects. Their style, however, of choosing which projects to work on and how to interleave them, is very individual, ranging from monochronic to polychronic preferences. Chapter 4 presents empirical results of multitasking behavior in real-world information work environments. But first, Chapter 3 discusses what might contribute to multitasking with digital media.

# CHAPTER 3

# What Contributes to Multitasking?

In Chapter 1, I wrote about the abundance of information available in our digital age. Yet the unimaginable amount of information alone is not the cause of multitasking when working on the computer. Rather, in my view I see it as one of many other factors that facilitate multitasking. Certainly we might expect that the more information available (and accessible), the more opportunities exist to switch and view different information sources. McLuhan (1994) spoke about how the communication medium changes how people perceive. The rise of the print medium led people to perceive the world in a format that was consistent with the rectangular printed page. The rise of the Internet, along with the interface design of computers has also led to behaviors that reflect, and at times even mimic, the design of these media. To unpack why people multitask, I present a range of factors that could contribute to leading people to multitask, as summarized in Table 3.1.

| Table 3.1: Factors that contribute to multitasking behavior when using digital media | |
|---|---|
| Contributing factor | Effect on multitasking |
| Abundance of information available | Large choice of information to access |
| Number of tasks/projects | More projects increase the chance of switching |
| Size of workplace social networks | More opportunities for interactions, interruptions |
| Ease and speed of accessing information | Low cost, low barriers, to accessing information |
| The computer interface | Display of potential information to access; affords hypermediacy |
| The structure of hypermedia | Different access points to a concept; the structure of nodes and links maps onto an associative trail of thought |
| Cultural assumptions with technology | Evolving social norms with digital media use, e.g., rapid response, increased availability |
| Physical arrangement of office space | Physical collocation leads to higher interruptions |

## 3.1    ABUNDANCE OF INFORMATION AVAILABLE

Chapter 1 described the amount of information that people consume on a daily basis. Milgrim (1970) wrote that people adapt to information overload by devoting a shorter duration to each source of information. There is indeed an opportunity cost to dealing with information. Information workers have a finite number of hours in the workplace, and considering the capability to work outside of the workplace, there is a finite number of hours in the day. Considering just the time in the workplace, the more information one deals with in the workplace, the less time one has to devote to any particular piece of information. I invite the reader to do a Gedanken experiment. A wealth of information does not necessarily *require* that one has to attend a shorter duration to each information source. One can in principle still maintain focus on a piece of information, essentially ignoring the other information. One could thus finish a task or even subtask through to completion before turning to do something else.

I maintain that the sheer amount of information available is thus not a sufficient reason alone to cause multitasking. Even before the Internet, people could access information through television, the radio, newspapers, books, magazines, letters, and face-to-face. Information abundance is not new. The Internet has exponentially increased the amount of information available to the individual; however people could still work monochronically independent of the amount of information available and accessible.

## 3.2    NUMBER OF TASKS AND PROJECTS IN WHICH PEOPLE ARE INVOLVED

The number of projects that people are involved in can also affect multitasking. In our research, we found that information workers average working on 12 different projects within the same time period (Gonzalez and Mark, 2004). Projects done in the workplace can be work related or personal. Each project has its own time pressures (e.g., deadlines for milestones), but also its own set of subtasks and operations involved in working on the subtasks. In addition, each project has its own constellation of people associated with it. So, the more projects, the more different subtasks, the more different types of operations that can be done (e.g., email, document editing), and the more people there are with who to interact. The corollary is that as the number of projects for someone grows in number, there is a larger circle of people who can potentially interrupt, either electronically, by phone or face-to-face. Simply due to probability, as the number of projects that people are involved in increases, people have a greater chance of switching to another subtask, operation, or person, simply because there are a higher number of them. In fact, the relationship of number of projects and multitasking was shown empirically. In a study of 32 information workers, we found that the more projects in which a person was involved, the more often they checked email and Facebook (Mark et al., 2015). This held true whether we look at switching applications or switching between

Internet sites. An interpretation is that the more projects one has, the more switching that one does between projects, and then it follows that there exist more opportunities for checking Facebook and email while switching.

## 3.3    SIZE OF WORKPLACE SOCIAL NETWORKS

A related idea to the number of tasks one is involved in is that the size of one's workplace social network could be related to the amount of multitasking. The larger one's social network in the workplace, the more opportunities one has for interactions, and consequent potential interruptions. Enterprise social networking sites, being adopted increasingly more in organizations, differ from other types of organizational communication in that they make one's network in the organization visible (boyd, 2010). Thus, enterprise social networking sites can serve as markers, or external representations of the relationships employees have developed with each other in the workplace. However, social networking sites are more than markers. They reveal information about workplace relationships: significant correspondence was found with the amount of social networking site usage and employees' ratings of how close they were with each other in the organization (Wu et al., 2010). We would thus expect that larger social networks would provide more opportunities for people to communicate with others, see updates, and glean information about others and about the workplace. This is due to network effects; the more people in a network, the more value the network (or social media site) has for the user, for gaining resources such as social capital. Of course the consequence is that with larger social networks there are more sources and opportunities for distractions and interruptions from other people.

Some indirect evidence shows this relation. In a study conducted in a large global enterprise with over 400,000 employees, we investigated the role of social network size (Mark et al., 2014c). The organization employed a social media application platform behind its firewall. We examined the patterns of over 20,000 users of the most active users of the social media platform. Counter-intuitively, we found that there is an *inverse* relationship between the size of one's social network (as measured by the number of friends in the social networking site and how highly regarded that person is by others in the organization. In other words, the smaller one's network in the organization (the fewer friends one has in their online enterprise social network), then the *higher* one was assessed by colleagues. One potential explanation was that "friending" in an enterprise might be considered frivolous or non work-related, which could explain the negative relation with high assessment. However, another explanation, and one that would need to be tested, is that the larger the social network size, the more time is spent in upkeep of the network. The more time spent in upkeep, the less time spent in organizational work which could explain why those with larger network sizes were judged to have lower expertise and lower reputation in the organization. It also follows that the larger the network, the more time spent in distractions and interruptions that occur, leaving less time to develop expertise. This interpretation seems to make sense as social networks require maintenance: social network sites are used to maintain weak ties as well as strong ties (Castells, 2003). Thus, the larger the network size, the more likely it could be that people are interrupted and consequently multitask more.

## 3.4    THE EASE AND SPEED OF ACCESSING INFORMATION

The notion of remediation is described by Bolter and Grusin (2000) as when a new media improves upon another prior one. The development of the Internet (and World Wide Web) has improved upon the constraint of slowness of the print medium by making access to information immediate. In considering the notion of access very broadly, as Borgman (2000) does, access involves network connectivity, user skills, and content. With the Internet, never before in history have we had the means to access information so rapidly, but especially so effortlessly. Provided one has an Internet connection and basic computer skills, information can be retrieved in milliseconds. As an illustration, before the Internet, to find a fact one had to go to the Encyclopedia Britannica, or to the library, or look up the fact in a journal or book. This of course took time. With digital search, facts are near instantaneously available, yet of course one has to sift through the results to find relevant facts. Prior to the Internet, to contact another person, one could telephone, write a letter, or travel to meet them in person. Now, with electronic communication, people can use synchronous forms of communication such as text chat, Skype, Facebook, or use other forms of social media to contact another or to even broadcast to the crowd to ask for information. Even email, an asynchronous communication medium, often becomes synchronous in near-real time. One can also subscribe to blogs, newsfeeds, Twitter feeds, etc., to receive information. The Internet has reduced the cost of accessing information but also has largely removed the barrier of information access. Thus, the ease of accessing information opens the floodgates of information flow.

The desire for immediate access of information is an historical theme in the development of media (Bolter and Grusin, 2000). The invention of the telegraph, telephone, radio, and television all made access to others and to information immediate. However, as the concept of remediation implies, media can always be improved upon leading us closer and closer to achieving immediacy of information access. Immediacy of information is seductive; we need no longer wait to find facts or to satisfy whims of interest. We can immediately get to the information we need, as a thought springs up and while it is still in short-term memory.

## 3.5    THE COMPUTER INTERFACE

The design of the personal computer interface affords what Bolter and Grusin (2000) refer to as hypermediacy. Hypermediacy refers to heterogeneous representations of information. The availability of multiple windows overlapping on the interface provides external representations of information that compete for attention. As the user's thoughts shift, a click can bring another window into the forefront of the user's view and thus immediately solidify the new direction of thought. But what is actually happening is that the user is oscillating between an awareness of the interface and an awareness of content. So as the user switches between different windows, the user is experiencing shifts of attention between content, then briefly attends again to the interface as the user searches and clicks on another window, and then back attending to content.

The multiplicity of windows arranged on the interface displays a variety of potential information available to the user. While one window is in focus, the surrounding windows always contain information that remains at the periphery of one's attention. A click can bring the window to the foreground (or in full view), thus bringing to focus that information contained within. As the user clicks on different windows, information oscillates between being in the foreground and background of attention. When clicks are fast, although information may not even have a chance to spring to the user's full focus of attention, sensory traces could be processed (cf. Sakitt, 1976).

Not only are documents within applications easily accessible, but so are varied applications such as email, productivity apps (Word, Excel, PowerPoint), and social media. Again, although one window is brought to the foreground, the other windows, representing different tasks, or subtasks, exist in the periphery and can provide prompts to retrieve information contained in the applications or documents. A click to bring a window to the forefront is nearly effortless for the user. Thus, the design of the computer interface, enabling the visibility of multiple windows, makes multitasking an easy process.

## 3.6    THE STRUCTURE OF HYPERMEDIA

Hypermedia was originally conceived of as a system for organizing the loosely structured information of the Web. Vannevar Bush's original idea of the Memex, which is the forerunner to the hypermedia of the Web, was based on a method of organizing information that would follow the associative trails of ideas which is the process by how people retrieve concepts (Bush, 1945). There are many different access points to a concept. If a person wants to try and recall the name of Herzog's documentary film about the German pilot who became a prisoner during the Vietnam war one might search through their mind for associations using "Vietnam," or "soldier," or "airplane," as tag words (the film is *Little Dieter Needs to Fly*). But hypermedia works the other way as well. Coming across a concept, for example by reading a news article, can evoke another related idea in one's memory through association. On the Internet, the structure of nodes and links make it easy to follow this associative trail of thought. If people come across a word or image that evokes another thought, it is easy to quickly access the other thought, through hyperlinks or web search. Web pages are structured to enable ease of access of other thoughts. When one reads a Wikipedia page, hyperlinks can quickly direct one to another Wikipedia page to follow up on an interesting thought. People can get lost in Wikipedia, pursuing different paths. Unfortunately, there is not an Ariadne golden thread to lead us quickly back to where we started. What we do have are back buttons that we click until we return to the original page. However, by the time we have clicked on our third, fourth, or nth link, we may have forgotten about the original page. Thus, Vannevar Bush's idea of hypermedia was in response to the artificiality of information storage and categorization at the time, using constrained indexing systems. His proposal to shift to a mechanism that would more closely map onto human thinking was adopted in the design of the Web. Indeed, it is easy to pursue associations and this ease may contribute to interruptions and thus multitasking.

A related hypothesis concerns the idea that hypermedia may have deeper influences in us than we realize. When we use the Internet we are accustomed to working in a hypermedia format. To Millennials who grew up with the Internet, the hypermedia format may be more second nature than to older generations. Although paper books are still by and large written in a linear format, more and more, publications, especially ebooks, and articles on the Web, are structured in a hypermedia format, providing links for concepts, names, and terms. It is very possible then that our experience with working in a hypermedia context has led us to develop habits of pursuing associations quite readily. Eliza Dresang wrote about *Radical Change*, the idea that digital media has led to new forms in children's literature (Dresang, 1999). She observed that children's literature has become more nonlinear. The hypermedia structure is influencing a whole new generation.

## 3.7    CULTURAL ASSUMPTIONS WITH TECHNOLOGY

The invention of technology historically has served to speed up the pace of work. A few examples include the telegraph, which speeded the transmission of news; the typewriter which led to faster written messages; the telephone, which enabled synchronous communication, the invention of the airplane, and later jet, which speeded up the delivery of mail (the first U.S. scheduled airmail service was in 1918), and the database, which enabled us to store information to speed up access to data. Internet technologies such as email have sped up not only the transmission speed of information but also have increased the pure volume of written communication. It is estimated that 183 billion emails were sent daily worldwide in 2013 (Radicati Group, Inc., 2013). But the rise of email has been accompanied by a revision of cultural norms surrounding online communication. With email, there is the expectation that one will respond to a message with rapidity, perhaps following the same trend of the sender's intent of speed. This had led to a cycle where people keep checking email—to make sure that an important message is not missed (and which must be rapidly responded to) as many of our informants in our studies claim.

The cultural assumptions accompanying interruptions have evolved with digital media. Taking a phone call while face-to-face with another person used to not be an acceptable norm. With the ubiquity of mobile phones, cultural norms have changed surrounding their use. There is no clearer example than the scenario where it is not unusual anymore to see people on a date while both are texting others who are remote. Or young people will stand in a group, checking email and texting instead of making eye contact and conversing with each other. In the workplace, the notion of self-interrupting to check Facebook or email is not considered abnormal behavior. People have always taken work breaks. But in current information work environments, the breaks can occur rapidly while sitting at one's desk. Another cultural norm that has evolved with smartphone and personal computer use is the culture of availability. It is expected that with mobile devices employees are available to answer calls and messages beyond work hours and during home life (Mazmanian et al., 2013).

## 3.8    PHYSICAL ARRANGEMENT OF OFFICE SPACE

It is not just digital media that can lead to multitasking but also the physical setting where one works. Open office plans are intentionally designed to foster interaction whereas individual offices are designed to enable privacy, to "shut off" the rest of the workplace. Considering then that an open office environment affords people the opportunity to "talk through the cubicle walls" and quickly visit others' cubicles, it would seem that people working in collocated settings would be interrupted by colleagues more frequently. More interruptions would lead to more multitasking. We conducted a shadowing study in high tech companies where we closely observed interruptions (Mark et al., 2005). We divided the informants in this study into two categories: *collocated*, where their office exists in a cubicle in an open office environment and where they had at least one of their team-members sitting in an adjacent cubicle, i.e., sharing a wall, or *distributed*, where their workspace was physically separated from their teammates by being at a distance from them in an enclosed office, across the room, or in another building. Fifteen people were collocated and nine were distributed. We found that physical collocation did show a significant effect. We found that collocated people experienced significantly more segments of their projects interrupted compared to those who were distributed. Therefore, collocated workers, compared to distributed workers, are more likely to switch their attention due to interruptions as opposed to completing work on that task. Our observations can help to explain this. Awareness of when to interrupt collocated colleagues due to overhearing them was commonly observed and described during interviews. Informants listened to what their cubicle neighbors were doing and avoided interrupting them when they were busy. However, when they sensed that their colleagues were available, then they interrupted them. When in doubt, they asked if they could interrupt. The questions and comments for their colleague were often stored up so that when the person became available multiple interruptions from people occurred. The open office environment affords a culture of participation even when people are not directly asked for advice. In our studies, informants described that they overheard problems that their colleagues faced, which drew them in to offer help. The informants explained that they were on alert to offer their expertise to their colleagues.

A serious pursuit of multitasking raises two questions. First, have people always multitasked? As *in situ* multitasking was never measured prior to the studies that I will present, it is not possible to definitively answer this. However, my guess is yes, that people have always multitasked. Telephones interrupted people in the workplace, as did colleagues, leading people to shift attention to a new topic. People worked on multiple tasks and had competing demands and deadlines. But this leads to the second question: prior to the widespread use of the personal computer and Internet, have people multitasked to the extent that they do at present? Again, we cannot answer this definitively as detailed multitasking was never measured. However, we do have a clue to this answer from early tracking studies of managers, where they were shadowed throughout their workday, and which showed a change in how managers distributed their time over the course of the day.

The first five columns on the left in Table 3.2 show data from shadowing studies of managers in the years 1965–1992, before email was in widespread popular use in many companies. The Internet was also not in widespread use. The two right columns show data of shadowing studies from the years 2002 and 2006, when both email and the Internet were in popular use in companies. There are two striking differences from the pre and post email shadowing studies. The first difference is that the percentage of time spent in deskwork nearly doubled on average. Before email, approximately 23% of the day was spent in deskwork by managers. This percentage grew to an average of 42.5% with the advent of email.

The second noteworthy difference is the amount of time spent in scheduled meetings. Prior to email, the average time from the first five studies is that 40% of the day was spent in scheduled meetings (phone or face-to-face). Yet after email, the average time spent in scheduled meetings, from the latter two studies, is 21%, about half the time. Together, these two results suggest the hypothesis that with the rise of email, more work that was formerly done in scheduled meetings, is now done at the desk. Perhaps problems were solved, or information gathered through email, desktop conferencing, or the Internet. Thus, while we cannot answer whether people multitasked to the same extent prior to email and the Internet that they do currently, the data does suggest that people distributed their time differently over the course of the day. Prior to the adoption of the Internet and email in organizations, with more time in scheduled meetings (where norms of interaction dictate that attention be paid) and less time spent with deskwork (where one can distribute their attention as they please), it is likely that there was simply less chance to do multitasking. In the next chapter, I will describe multitasking behavior of information workers *in situ*.

Table 3.2: A comparison of *in situ* workplace studies showing time distribution of work activities

| | Horne & Lupton 1965[a] | Mintzberg 1970[a] | Sproull 1984[a] | Ives & Olson 1981[a] | Stephens et al. 1992 | Hudson et al. 2002[b] | Mark & Gonzalez 2004 |
|---|---|---|---|---|---|---|---|
| Deskwork | 26% | 22% | 19% | 19% | 28% | 42% | 42.9% |
| Phone | 9 | 6 | 13 | 9 | 9 | — | 7.6 |
| Scheduled Meetings | 10 | 59 | 34 | 48 | 48 | 27 | 14.3 |
| Un-Sched. Meetings | 55 | 10 | 34 | 20 | 14 | 19 | 22.3 |
| Other | — | 3 | — | 2 | 2 | — | 12.9 |
| Total Time | 100% | 100% | 100% | 100% | 100% | 88% | 100% |

CHAPTER 4

# Multitasking in Information Work

In our current digital age, working on multiple activities is an inherent nature of much information work. In academia we are tasked with supervising students, serving on committees, teaching, writing grants, being involved in the broader research community such as reviewing, and of course, participating in multiple research projects. In start-ups, employees typically wear multiple hats, often changing tasks as varied as financial operations, project management, marketing, and programming. In large complex organizations, information work as well typically involves participating in multiple projects, initiatives and teams. By information work, I refer to work where the primary focus is on managing information. This can be creating, seeking, synthesizing, modifying, and especially communicating information. Although information work has been distinguished from knowledge work, my main thrust is on how people switch between different activities and this occurs irrespective of the nature of the information.

Information work has been examined from different perspectives. A number of different fields have set about to do task modeling of information work, using dimensions such as degree of person involvement, complexity, cognitive load, and task characteristics, mostly in experimental laboratory settings (cf. Campbell, 1988, for a review). However, this body of literature fails to consider how tasks are conducted in actual real-world environments. In real settings, people generally do not work in monochronic patterns. Tasks are fragmented, with people switching between different tasks. The fragmentation in turn impacts a number of factors concerning workplace behavior, mood and attitudes. It is hard to simulate all the different factors that might affect multitasking when using a laboratory setting.

Early on, we set out to understand how task switching occurs in a real-world context. Early studies of time distribution among managers were done in real-world office environments (e.g., Horneand Lupton, 1965; Mintzberg, 1970; Sproull, 1984). These studies were done in the age before personal computers and certainly before the Internet entered the workplace in commonplace usage. The nature of information work since then went through a radical change and by the year 2000, information workers were already working in very technology-rich environments.

More and more, studies are providing empirical evidence that information workers engage in multiple activities in the workplace. Studies of managers documented how they work on multiple tasks (Czerwinski et al., 2004; Hudson et al., 2002; Mintzberg, 1973; Sproull, 1984). The demands of the workplace in managing these multiple tasks lead people to work in polychronic patterns. Studies have also described how the work of information workers is characterized by spending short amounts of time in tasks and switching frequently (Czerwinski et al., 2004; Hudson et al.,

2002; Gonzalez and Mark, 2004). This has been found not only with managers as described above but also with software developers (Perlow, 1999), telecommuters (Jackson, 2002), financial analysts, and admins (Gonzalez and Mark, 2004).

As discussed earlier in Chapter 3, working with digital media can influence how people work on multiple tasks. I described how the rapid access to a wide range of information, as well as the design of the personal computer interface of displaying multiple windows, can contribute to activity switching. To add to the complexity of managing information work, workers also use a variety of digital and physical devices to conduct their work: computers and smart phones, but also still paper documents. Further, information workers use a range of applications in work, switching between email, productivity apps (Word, Excel, etc.), social media, communication software, and others.

## 4.1    WORK FRAGMENTATION

When people work on multiple tasks in a polychronic manner, their work becomes fragmented. I consider *work fragmentation* as a break in continuous work activity. Work fragmentation has two main aspects: (1) the length of time people spend in a continuous activity and (2) interruptions of that activity. In general, we can consider that work is more fragmented the shorter amount of time one spends on a task (without completing the task), and the more interruptions one has. This chapter will focus on the length of time that people spend in an activity while the next chapter will focus on interruptions of activity.

It is important to consider that task switching may be beneficial at times. It could serve to refresh one if tired, and can provide new ideas. Working on one task can lead to new thinking about a similar task through analogy. On the other hand, too much task switching with too many different activities could be detrimental. It often requires a start-up time to orient oneself to an activity. Spending too short of a time at one stretch in a complex project could result in not accomplishing very much.

Task switching can be triggered by interruptions. Although interruptions can often bring relevant information for one's work, in many cases, resuming work after an interruption involves a cognitive cost to reorient to the task. Interruptions can also become nested, as one interrupts one task to work on another, and in turn one then interrupts that task to work yet on something else. This chain of interruptions can lead to stress as one strives to keep track of multiple states of tasks. Yet while interruptions have been proven to induce stress (Mark et al., 2008), it is not only interruptions that tax an individual, but also the process of frequently switching activities.

## 4.2    MEASURING MULTITASKING ACTIVITY *IN SITU*

Considering multitasking in information work as both online and offline activity poses a challenge to measurement. Benbunan-Fich et al. (2011) constructed a metric of multitasking that provides a measure of switching and overlap of tasks. These metrics were based on self-reports of computer usage and measured work done on the computer. However, self-reports are subject to bias and often fail to ask participants to consider the switching that is done between online and offline work. Observational approaches that are ethnographic or sensor-based can provide more accurate representations of task switching in actual work environments.

The data reported here on multitasking is from Gonzalez and Mark (2004) and Mark et al. (2005). The studies were done by observing information workers in the course of their actual work, at three different high tech companies. The methodology used to understand this *in situ* multitasking was a "shadowing" observation technique similar to those used in previous time management studies (Mintzberg, 1970; Sproull, 1984). The researcher observed the informant in her cubicle or office, and followed the informant around the workplace. Every action that the informant performed (e.g., opening a Word document, making a phone call, or interacting with a colleague) was measured to the second by the observer using a stopwatch. To the extent possible, details of the action were noted. Data was recorded in an activity tracking log, based on Mintzberg's structured observation method (Mintzberg, 1970). Thirty-six people in total were observed, each person for a period of three and a half days. The first half-day was used to become familiar with their activities and working style. It was also done so that the informant could become used to the presence of the observer. For the next three days, all the informants' activities were recorded, averaging 26 h per informant. Post-observation in-depth interviews were also conducted.

It is always a concern in ethnographic observation that the observer's presence may influence the informant. We cannot rule out this possibility. However, in real-work environments, information workers have to react to the demands of the workplace. Whether or not they may try to act differently when first observed, very soon they become used to the observer's presence and settle in to their work routine.

Most people observed worked in cubicles in an open office environment; three had their own offices. This kind of open office setting allows team members to interact and communicate easily with other colleagues even without the need to move from their own cubicles. It is common that people chat with each other through the walls, or even walk over to join conversations in other cubicles. At the same time, the height of the cubicles was high enough to provide privacy for the occupants. The employees generally concentrated on their work within the cubicle.

## 4.3    MULTITASKING: SWITCHING EVENTS

As one might imagine in most high technology companies, the workplace was characterized as a very fast-paced environment with multiple conversations, telephones ringing constantly and people walking unannounced into others' cubicles or "chatting through the walls." The work of the employees was characterized by a constant switching among physical and digital artifacts as well. Their work could be described as chains of short-term events.

| Events | % entire day | Avg. Time/Day (sd) | Avg. Time/Event (sd) |
|---|---|---|---|
| Table 4.1: Average continuous time spent on events before switching (hour:min:sec). N=14 | | | |
| Using phone[1] | 5.83 | 0:30:22 (0:19:14) | 0:02:25 (0:00:42) |
| Using email | 9.17 | 0:47:46 (0:21:18) | 0:02:22 (0:00:27) |
| Using PCs[2] | 29.48 | 2:33:36 (1:11:23) | 0:02:53 (0:01:10) |
| Using paper documents/ books | 6.80 | 0:35:25 (0:29:48) | 0:01:47 (0:00:31) |
| Using other tools[3] | 0.31 | 0:01:38 (0:03:08) | 0:01:04 (0:00:15) |
| Talking through the walls | 2.94 | 0:15:18 (0:14:12) | 0:01:40 (0:00:24) |
| Interacting with people in their own cubicle | 6.88 | 0:35:53 (0:29:25) | 0:03:34 (0:01:57) |
| Formal meetings | 14.39 | 1:14:58 (1:17:40) | 0:41:47 (0:12:46) |
| Going to other cubicles | 9.11 | 0:47:29 (0:27:21) | 0:07:37 (0:03:24) |
| Other (unknown, personal) | 15.09 | 1:18:39 (0:34:26) | 0:17:27 (0:06:27) |
| **All events except "Formal meetings" and "Other"** | **70.52%** | **0:45:56 (0:52:03)** | **0:03:08 (0:02:27)** |
| **All events total** | **100%** | **0:52:07 (0:55:25)** | **0:08:55 (0:13:23)** |

[1] Includes time spent on cell phones
[2] Includes both PCs and financial terminals – does not include email
[3] "Other tools" include: handheld calculator, planners, and address books

In Chapter 2, I discussed that multitasking can be viewed at different levels of granularity. It is possible to focus on switching between different "low-level" operations, such as speaking on the phone, working on a Word document, or doing email. At a more course granularity, it is possible to focus on switching between projects. At a fine-grained granularity, we define these "low-level" events in work as *any continuous use of a device or engagement in an interaction with other individuals* (e.g., phone conversation, using an electronic spreadsheet, writing Word documents). Following work by Lee Sproull (1984) who shadowed managers in the 1980's before the personal computer was widely used in the workplace, we considered that in any particular event neither the structure nor the content changes. Interactions were also considered events, such as conversing in the hallway, in one's office, or, in the case of people in cubicles, talking "through the wall."

Table 4.1 shows the average time spent on any event per person, per day, for all three roles combined: analysts, developers, and managers (from Gonzalez and Mark, 2004). What was most surprising to us was the short amount of time that these information workers spent on an event before another event is initiated. We left out of our calculation: 1) formal meetings, as we reasoned that people are "prisoners" when in a meeting (with the team leader or manager usually the warden), the length determined by factors beyond their control, and also 2) "other" events (personal and unknown). The data showed that people spent on the average slightly over *three minutes* on any event (3 min, 5 s) before switching to another event or being interrupted. Our data reveal that multi-tasking is done to an extent even far more than we realized: every three minutes on the average people switched events throughout their workday. There were no significant differences between analysts, developers, and managers for all but two of the events. We found that the three roles differ significantly in the continuous time spent using the computer, and a post hoc test showed that developers spend significantly more time using a personal computer compared with managers (about one minute more). Four minutes on the personal computer before being interrupted or switching events is still, however, quite a short period of time for developers.

In a study done by Norman Su, doing a similar shadowing technique with high-tech information workers, he found that the average length of time when doing solitary work was actually shorter: 2 min, 31 s. In fact, considering just communication acts alone (email, telephone, instant message) the average length of time spent on these events was even shorter: 2 min, 18 s (Su and Mark, 2008). The difference from the three minute average found by Gonzalez and Mark (2004) could be due to the fact that the study reported in Su and Mark was done four years later where there may have been a higher usage of the Internet and Internet communication applications such as instant message. A later shadowing study done in 2012 of information workers revealed that they averaged even shorter amounts of time on any event just considering work done on the computer: averaging 1 min, 15 s (Mark et al., 2012).

## 4.4    MULTITASKING AMONG DEVICES

If we now just look at the usage of the different information artifacts, we can clearly see a pattern of short-term usage duration. Table 4.2 (from Gonzalez and Mark, 2004) shows the length of time that people spent using different electronic devices and paper documents before they were interrupted or switched to another activity. Clearly, people spend the most time per day working on the computer. Next in line is phone use and paper artifacts, although these involve much less time than computer usage.

| Table 4.2: Average time usage per device per person (hour:min:sec) | | | | |
|---|---|---|---|---|
| Device | % entire day | % of device usage only | Avg. Time/Day (sd) | Avg. Time/ Event (sd) |
| PC[1] | 37.01 | 72.37 | 3:12:52 (1:13:48) | 0:02:52 (0:00:51) |
| Financial terminals[2] | 1.64 | 3.19 | 0:16:59 (0:13:13) | 0:01:20 (0:00:36) |
| Paper documents and formats | 5.01 | 8.92 | 0:26:06 (0:22:21) | 0:01:33 (0:00:28) |
| Books, manual and other references | 1.79 | 3.50 | 0:09:20 (0:12:16) | 0:01:57 (0:00:55) |
| Hand-held calculator[3] | 0.05 | 0.10 | 0:01:13 (0:01:29) | 0:00:48 (0:00:18) |
| Daily-Monthly planner (paper)[3] | 0.19 | 0.38 | 0:04:40 (0:04:18) | 0:00:50 (0:00:15) |
| Address books (paper)[3] | 0.07 | 0.14 | 0:01:45 (0:03:04) | 0:01:00 (0:00:42) |
| Phone unit | 5.16 | 10.08 | 0:26:52 (0:18:23) | 0:02:17 (0:00:43) |
| Cell Phone | 0.67 | 1.31 | 0:04:53 (0:06:06) | 0:04:13 (0:04:24) |
| **All devices[4]** | **51.59%** | **100%** | **0:44:57 (1:13:27)** | **0:02:11 (0:01:52)** |

[1] Includes using email
[2] Only seven informants have terminals
[3] Only three informants used each of these
[4] Weighted average

Thus, if we focus on switching between devices and artifacts, i.e., excluding human interaction, then we find that people spent an average of 2 min 11 s working with any device or paper before they switched to another device. There was a significant difference in phone use by people's work role: developers speak significantly less time on the phone per day than analysts or managers, as we might expect. Thus, if we consider activity switching in terms of attention, people devote a very short amount of their attention on any device or artifact before switching to something else. Reorienting to some types of devices or applications takes a shorter amount of time than others. But imagine the case when one intends to work on a Word document that is not already open on the screen. There is some cognitive effort spent in locating the file in one's computer, opening it, and then orienting to the place where one left off (or creating a new document to work on).

Thus, the work of attention workers is characterized by switching attention throughout the day. No matter whether we focus on attention switching in communication, among different artifacts, between online and offline activity, or the whole picture, the data show that attention is fragmented in real information work.

## 4.5    WORKING SPHERES

Our data so far conveys the very short-term nature of interactions with people and devices, and shows how people constantly switch between different events. In formal interviews and informal comments, the informants confirmed this behavior as typical in their day. However, this view of attention switching is at a fine-grained granularity in terms of events, as we defined them. But maybe switching between events is not so bad if they all involve the same project? As an academic, when I work on a research paper I am constantly switching between writing, reading articles, speaking with colleagues, and doing analyses. After all, I am still thinking about the same topic—it is just that the detailed low-level operations change. As long as these all concern the same project, then perhaps switching may not be so problematic. Or is it?

With Victor Gonzalez, we decided to next examine activity switching at a higher level of granularity, such as projects, which are comprised of the separate events described in Table 4.1. In the observations, it became clear that the participants referred to their activities in terms of very distinct bounds. For example, the informants would refer to project names, either formal or informal, or would use keywords to refer to projects. From studying the observation logs as well as other data collected, such as paper artifacts and transcripts, emerged the concept of *working sphere*, which describes higher levels of units of work or activities that people divide their work into on a daily basis. Interviews confirmed that people tended to consider and organize their work in terms of these higher-level aggregations of events, i.e., working spheres (Gonzalez and Mark, 2004).

A working sphere can roughly be thought of as a project. However, whereas projects are defined as temporary endeavors (Schwalbe, 2007), working spheres can be permanent ongoing activities such as routine checking of equipment, such as servers, or handling customer problems. We define a working sphere as a set of interrelated events, which share a common motive (or goal), involves the communication or interaction with a particular set of people, uses its own set of resources (e.g., communication tools, shared folder systems) and has its own time framework. With respect to tools, each working sphere might involve different documents, reference materials, software, or hardware. Working spheres are distinct. In academia, we may typically have unique working spheres of different research projects, courses that we teach, committee work, and paper reviewing. The unit of analysis of working sphere differs from the unit of work used by Czerwinski et al. (2004) who focused on the interruption of generic tasks such as email and phone calls. When we consider the fragmentation of work, the units we refer to are actually *working sphere segments*—single events or clusters of events that are part of a particular working sphere. The concept of working sphere has also been used to explain collaborative technology adoption, i.e., at the level of the group as a unit (Mark and Poltrock, 2004). Groups need to adopt a common collaborative technology when working in a particular working sphere in order to communicate and exchange information.

Thus, a working sphere is bounded by dimensions: the task, the people involved, the timeline, and in the course of real work, people distinguish their working spheres from one another. Further, people are typically involved in multiple spheres of work. Working spheres can also include activities not directly associated with one's work in the workplace such as planning a company picnic or organizing a fundraising campaign. Working spheres can be short term such as preparing a proposal, or long term, such as developing a new software system. Working spheres can also be personal—planning a daughter's birthday party. We next focused our analysis on how people switched among working spheres, i.e., units of work viewed at a higher level of granularity for which events such as phone calls or email are a subcomponent.

### 4.5.1    CENTRAL AND PERIPHERAL WORKING SPHERES

We expected that working spheres might be treated differently depending if one has primary responsibility for it or not. In other words, if one is accountable for the results of a working sphere, then they may behave differently with it than if they would not be accountable. As working spheres are generally shared with others, the same working sphere can be the primary responsibility for one person and at the same time can exist as peripheral work for another person. We thus identified two levels of engagement with a working sphere: central and peripheral. A working sphere is *central* to a person when it is of primary importance for an individual and they have some responsibility for it or are accountable for its outcome; otherwise it is *peripheral*. A peripheral working sphere might involve providing expertise, doing small tasks, or providing feedback. Often people are drawn into others' central working spheres to give advice or help out with a problem; these would be peripheral for the one who is giving the advice.

Working spheres can change in their priorities for people. When a working sphere suddenly becomes urgent, for example due to an unforeseen problem, then it suddenly springs into the forefront of one's attention while other working spheres recede into the background. For a system administrator, when the network goes down, then what was formerly routine maintenance immediately becomes a top priority for solving the problem.

Using a variety of sources of information, including asking informants to validate the working spheres in interviews, the number of working spheres in which each of our informants was involved in during the three days of observation was counted along with calculating the length of time they spent in each. Each person worked on an average of slightly over twelve working spheres per day, during the three days of observation. Note that a three-day "slice of time" was observed, so it is possible that an individual might work in additional working spheres that were not attended to in this three day period. Thus, it is quite possible that the average of twelve working spheres per person is an underestimate.

Table 4.3 shows that individuals work on more central than peripheral working spheres (from Gonzalez and Mark, 2004). They average about nine working spheres and three peripheral working spheres. Although people averaged about 34 min daily in each of their working spheres, it does not occur as a continuous period of time. Instead, people frequently switch between their different working spheres, spending small periods of time in *working sphere segments*. Table 4.3 shows that the actual average duration of a working sphere segment is quite short (10 min, 29 s). Individuals clearly spend more time in working spheres which are central to their work, averaging over 12 min at a stretch. People tend to spend much shorter periods of time in what are peripheral working spheres (about 5 1/2 min). Thus, even when we view multitasking in terms of a broader view of switching working spheres as opposed to a finer-grained view in terms of events, we find that people still switch working spheres rapidly, about every ten and a half minutes throughout the workday.

Table 4.3: Average number of working spheres (WS) per person, average time per WS segment, and avg. total time spent in each WS per day (hour:min:sec)

| Type of WS | Average # WS/day (sd) | Avg. Time/ WS segment (sd) | Avg. Total Time / WS segment (sd) |
|---|---|---|---|
| Central | 9.31 (4.99) | 0:12:16 (0:03:56) | 0:45:21 (0:19:38) |
| Peripheral | 2.90 (1.63) | 0:05:34 (0:03:43) | 0:08:18 (0:06:06) |
| **All** | **12.22 (5.30)** | **0:10:29 (0:02:51)** | **0:33:58 (0:12:04)** |

The informants developed strategies to manage the constant interruptions in their different working spheres. They created artifacts (paper or digital) as reminders of pending work, such as post-it notes, used their email inbox to create self-reminders, or made printouts of emails. The artifacts always appeared in a visible spot of their working space so that they served as reminders. For example, post-it notes were placed on the monitor, desk, or wall, or email printouts were on the desk in their field-of-view. The artifacts were flexible, as they were moved around, and reorganized as priorities in work changed. When the working sphere task was completed, the post-it note could be removed, or the email deleted. The use of these ad hoc strategies provided a quick overview of the state of particular working spheres. Yet, creating these artifacts also involved additional work to keep up with and manage the constant switching.

## 4.5.2    WORKING SPHERES WITHOUT "NONSIGNIFICANT" DISRUPTIONS

We noticed that our informants, sometimes while working in one working sphere, were interrupted by work from another working sphere, briefly switched to this second working sphere, and then resumed work in the first working sphere. Examples of this can be when somebody brings a document into the office for that person to sign, or when someone gets a quick phone call. We realized that some disruptions are not significant and would not introduce a large overhead to resume work. We conducted a further analysis of our data where we explored the effects of disregarding short distractions on the segment length. We used a criteria of two minutes after reviewing the data and decided that this would make a feasible heuristic with which to consider interruptions that were not very disruptive. We then coded the data also considering how much attention the disruption required. We thus removed interruptions of two minutes or less, i.e., that were short and judged not to be disruptive. We re-analyzed the data considering a working sphere segment as "continuous" even if people turned to another working sphere for less than two minutes. Even after removing what we considered "nonsignificant" disruptions, people still averaged only a short time in a working sphere segment (12 min, 18 s). The flip side to this result is that about every 12 min people are faced with a "significant" disruption that lasts 2 min or longer.

### 4.5.3    METAWORK

Individuals spent part of their day on a set of activities that is not connected with any specific working sphere but rather related to the management of all of them. We call these activities *metawork* (Gonzalez and Mark, 2004). People periodically conduct metawork throughout the day, which involves coordination, checking activities, organizing email, organizing their desk at the start or end of a working day, and catching up with teammates on what they have missed. The information workers we studied spend an average of 44 1/2 min per day conducting metawork, and similar to working spheres, this work is also conducted in shorter chunks averaging six and a half minutes at any one time. Generally, we found that individuals engage in metawork whenever they conclude large activities, or when they return from a meeting. Metawork is another means by which people can manage their multitasking. It enables them to get an overview of the state of their fragmented work.

### 4.5.4    WORK FRAGMENTATION AND TIME OF DAY

We next looked at how work is fragmented in the morning compared to the afternoon. Based on an examination of the data, we divided the data into morning (until 12 noon) and afternoon (after 1 p.m.). We did not consider data between noon and 1 p.m. as this is likely a lunch break.

First, there were no significant differences between numbers of interruptions that occurred in the morning or afternoon. However, working spheres in the morning (10 min, 72 s) had a significantly shorter duration than in the afternoon (14 min, 40 s), before being interrupted or before people switched to another working sphere (Mark et al., 2005). These differences in the duration of the working spheres over the course of the day suggest that people may be able to concentrate longer on work in the afternoon. As there were no differences in interruptions, it could be ruled out that more interruptions in the morning led to shorter working sphere lengths.

## 4.6    SUMMARY AND DISCUSSION: MULTITASKING AND FRAGMENTED WORK

Our results describe typical days for information workers. Our study confirms what many of our colleagues and ourselves have been informally observing for some time: that information work is very fragmented. Throughout their day, individuals are constantly moving from one topic to another and managing information streams from an array of sources. Table 4.4 presents a summary of the results of multitasking.

| Table 4.4: Summary of multitasking results | |
|---|---|
| **Work fragmentation** | **Length of time spent in continuous activity; interruptions of that activity** |
| Switching events | ranges from 1 min, 15 s to 3 min per event |
| Working spheres (WS) | avg. of 12 different WS; avg. time spent per WS: 10 min, 29 s |
| Central/peripheral WS | longer time spent per central WS (12 min, 16 s) than per peripheral WS (5 min, 34 s) |
| Metawork | avg. of 44 1/2 min per day; avg. of 6 1/2 min per instance |
| Switching devices | avg. of 2 min, 11 s per device |
| Time of day | WS segments are shorter in the morning |

What surprised us was exactly how fragmented the work is. In a typical day, we found that people spend an average of 3 min working on any single event (online and offline) before switching to another event. People spend the longest time in informal interactions, which average 4½ min each. Further, people spend a short amount at a time when they use artifacts, devoting their attention on the average to slightly more than 2 mins to any electronic device, application, or paper document before they switch to another activity. The longest duration of tool use is with personal computers as a whole, yet this averages only slightly more than 3 min at any one time.

While earlier I described how multi-tasking can be viewed at different levels of granularity, it is an advantage to understand how time is distributed among *working spheres*, activities that are thematically connected for the individual. In the course of their work people refer to their activities in terms of working spheres. Although they are switching among different events (e.g., email, phone calls) these events are representative of a working sphere. Working spheres can be central for a person, when one is accountable for the results; working spheres can also be peripheral, as when one is drawn in to other types of work to consult or help out. Working spheres are also highly fragmented: people spend on the average ten and a half minutes in continuous work on any sphere of work before they switch to another. Even after removing what we considered to be "nonsignificant" disruptions, we found that the length of time spent in a working sphere was not much longer on average. Working spheres are a useful concept to apply to understanding multitasking. When people switch to another activity, they conceptualize the activity in terms of a working sphere. In other words while the event may be creating a document, it is a document that is a part of a working sphere. Although they may be switching events, these events are contextually connected as a working sphere. It follows then that switching among different working spheres involves a larger cognitive shift then switching events within working spheres.

Most of our informants explained that their preference is to work in a single working sphere until the job is completed, i.e., to perform monochronic work. However, this is rarely the case because the data show that people switch their attention among different working spheres continually throughout the day. In the interviews, it was revealed that people develop strategies to adjust to the unpredictability of their environment, such as knowing they will need to respond to urgent requests (Mark et al., 2005).

Our work expands on the past studies of time distribution (Sproull, 1984; Mintzberg, 1973; Horne and Lupton, 1965) that looked only at managers' work in work environments before personal computers and Internet became in widespread use. Compared to these past studies we also examined the work of people in work roles other than managers, as well as analysts and software developers. Except for minor differences in personal computer use no significant differences existed in the fragmentation of their work. Switching between multiple working spheres is shown to be pervasive, affecting a range of information workers.

# CHAPTER 5

# Interruptions

People wanting to reduce their dependency on information technology can, for a large sum, pay to stay at an exclusive resort in the Costa Rican rainforest designed for people to vacation without using technology. The rainforest resort is far off the grid. This is a hefty price to pay for taking a break from using digital media. However, itt is not the only such resort available. Digital detox resorts have sprouted up in locations from the Samburu reserve in Kenya to the Trans-Himalaya to the Gobi desert in Mongolia. It is ironic that there is now a business market for digital-free vacations—paying to relinquish access to digital devices and information.

The intent of these resorts is that people pay for the opportunity to have a period of time where they can give up being interrupted by digital media, and then perhaps can even learn to reduce their dependency on digital media. One might consider that in such resorts people are replacing a focus on digital information to a focus on information from their natural surroundings. They are giving up an information-rich digital media environment. In the information workplace people can pull information from any computer file or the Internet or can receive push notifications from email, news, RSS feeds, social media, or can communicate by telephone, Skype, SMS or also simply face-to-face. People can switch their attention among a range of information sources—often triggered by interruptions.

Interruptions have been a target of study for over two decades in the HCI field. By and large, most studies of interruptions concerning digital media use (and also non-media use) were done in laboratory settings. There have been a few studies of information workers *in situ* (Czerwinski et al., 2004; Gonzalez and Mark, 2004; Rouncefield et al., 1994). Laboratory studies have focused on identifying characteristics of interruption effects such as the recovery of tasks after an interruption (Czerwinski et al., 2004; Iqbal and Horvitz, 2007), and timing of interruptions (Bailey and Iqbal, 2008; Adamczyk and Bailey, 2004). As more studies on interruptions are done, it raises questions on how interruptions affect people in a real-world work context. There is a range of influences that are difficult to model in a laboratory setting. For example, although the interruptions and the task can be controlled for, it is difficult to model aspects of work such as time pressure, the tasks that people are accountable for, relationships with colleagues, hierarchy and power in the workplace, career trajectories, and much more. This chapter discusses interruptions in the context of a real-world work environment.

Similar to switching tasks, interruptions can have both benefits as well as costs. Interruptions can be detrimental if they occur at inappropriate times (Czerwinski et al., 2004) or if they lead users to forget their main task focus (Cutrell et al., 2001). Although interruptions can often bring relevant information for one's work (Hudson et al., 2002; O'Connail and Frohlich, 1995), in many cases resuming work after an interruption involves a cognitive cost to reorient back to the task (Brumby et al., 2013). Interruptions can also become nested, leading to stress in keeping track of multiple states of tasks. Evidence suggests that fragmented work patterns negatively impact work productivity (Perlow, 1999).

These prior laboratory studies of interruptions have focused on descriptions of work tasks and characteristics of interruptions, such as frequency of occurrence. There remains, however, a number of questions about factors associated with interruptions, types of interruptions, and the effects that interruptions have on people. In this chapter I contribute to explaining *why* task switching and interruptions occur through identifying relevant factors in a real-world context. Guided by our observations and measurements, we realized that people's work fragmentation is affected by their interaction with others, how they are interrupted, their environment, and how their work is resumed. I examine the effects of working spheres, work role, communication, collocation, time of day, gender, personality, as well as the consequences of interruptions on resumption of the interrupted work and stress.

## 5.1    TYPES OF INTERRUPTIONS: EXTERNAL AND INTERNAL

Almost three decades ago, Miyata and Norman (1986) described that there are two basic types of interruptions. External interruptions are those that occur from some observable stimulus in the environment, such as a phone ringing, a colleague entering one's cubicle, or a notification from an email application. Internal, or self-interruptions, are those in which one stops a task of their own volition. From the observer's perspective, it is always interesting to watch a person self-interrupt. They may seem absorbed in a task and then suddenly for no apparent reason they stop what they are doing while in the middle of some operation and turn to do something else. In fact, since I have been working in this area, I have become hyper-aware of when I self interrupt—which is quite often.

Most studies of interruptions consider only external interruptions and neglect to address self-interruptions. But as I will discuss in this chapter, it is important to understand the differences between external and internal interruptions as they can have different effects on work. The environment likely affects the influence of external interruptions, for example whether one is in a closed office or open office environment. External and internal interruptions may affect whether and how fast work is resumed, and these interruption types can also have cross-influences.

As I described earlier, multitasking can be viewed with different lenses, at different levels of granularity. If we consider switching at the event level, then this can be triggered by either external or self-interruptions. People can also reach a break point in a task (Iqbal and Bailey, 2007) and switch events at this point. Examples of break points are finishing up a paragraph in a Word document, closing or leaving an application, finishing an email, sending it, and then leaving the application, leaving a face-to-face interaction, or finishing a phone call and hanging up the phone. A self-interruption would be considered to occur when one switches before a break point is reached. External interruptions are easier to detect by an observer than self-interruptions as the interruption or switching can be associated with the external stimulus. When viewed at the granularity of working spheres, both self-interruptions and external interruptions divide working spheres into working sphere segments.

In Table 5.1 we can see actions that resulted from both external and internal interruptions by information workers in high-tech environments, as found by Gonzalez and Mark (2004) (e.g., making a phone call or leaving the cubicle) as well as kinds of external interruptions (e.g., a person enters the cubicle). In fact, the data show that people interrupt themselves almost as often as they experience external interruptions. The most common external interruptions were due to verbal-based interruptions (such as visitors or phone calls) rather than to notification mechanisms from their e-mail or voice mail. Most self interruptions were due to people leaving their cubicle to interact with other individuals.

| Table 5.1: Average number and types of interruptions per day (Gonzalez and Mark, 2004) | | Average Interruptions per day (S.D) | % all types | Internal / External |
|---|---|---|---|---|
| **Internal** | Checking/using paper docs | 0.52 (0.86) | 1.87 | **49.11%** |
| | Checking/using computer | 1.54 (1.47) | 10.98 | |
| | Talking t/wall | 1.93 (2.15) | 6.89 | |
| | Phone call | 1.14 (1.56) | 4.09 | |
| | Email use | 1.04 (1.47) | 7.40 | |
| | Leaves cubicle | 5.00 (2.56) | 17.87% | |
| **External** | New email notif. | 3.55 (3.18) | 12.68% | **50.89%** |
| | Person arrives | 6.00 (3.03) | 21.45% | |
| | Status on terminals | 0.36 (0.82) | 1.28% | |
| | Phone ringing | 2.62 (2.01) | 9.36% | |
| | Voice message light | 0.19 (0.45) | 0.68% | |
| | Call through wall | 1.33 (1.75) | 4.77% | |
| | Reminder notification | 0.19 (0.40) | 0.68% | |
| **Total** | | 25.40 (8.23) | **100%** | **100%** |

### 5.1.1 SELF-INTERRUPTIONS

We don't know exactly why people self-interrupt. There can, in fact, be different reasons. People may self-interrupt to take a break. People may self-interrupt out of habit or may even be conditioned to self-interrupt. One reason that could explain some self-interruptions is that they occur when people need a problem to incubate. The nature of work for analysts and developers is generally intellective and when a problem is difficult to solve, incubation could help. As one analyst described and is reported in Gonzalez and Mark (2004), *"And even though you are not really spending time on [a problem], you are still sort of thinking about it in the background and understanding the relationships between different pieces of data or different business processes."* Thus, when one leaves a working sphere, it is always simmering still on the back burner.

An intriguing result is that people self-interrupt almost as often as they are externally interrupted. Previous observational work suggests that self-interruption is a function of the information environment, individual difference, habit, or routine (Jing and Dabbish, 2009). A later study by Dabbish et al. (2011) examined each of these influences in more detail. Dabbish et al. examined what task switch features were most closely associated with self-interruptions. They found that individuals were significantly more likely to self-interrupt to complete a solitary task (working with paper or on the computer) as opposed to engaging in a communication event such as face-to-face conversation, phone, or email.

Self-interruptions may, to some extent, be a function of external interruptions experienced. Some research suggests that there can be a lingering cognitive cost of interruptions that lasts longer than the actual interrupting event. This is known as "attentional residue," which refers to how cognitions of a task remain as a residue when one transitions to a subsequent task (Altman and Trafton, 2002; Leroy, 2002). It is unclear, however, whether the effect of "attentional residue" persists in a real-world work context where there are numerous additional stimuli demanding attention compared to a laboratory. Exposure to a lot of external interruptions could "break down" a person's attentional stamina, which could make them more vulnerable to self-interrupt. If the attentional residue effect persists, we would thus expect to see a positive temporal relationship between external interruptions and self-interruption.

This is exactly what was found. External interruptions in the previous hour significantly increased self-interruption in the next hour, with one additional external interruptions resulting in an 8% increase in self-interruption. At the same time, self-interruptions in the previous hour did not show an association with self-interruptions in the following hour. This result suggests that individuals may experience distraction as a function of external interruptions. One interpretation is that people may be conditioned to self-interrupt. By experiencing external interruptions they may become habituated to self-interrupt. However, time and external interruption accounted for only 4% of the variance in self-interruption suggesting their influence was minimal in comparison to individual differences (habit) and organizational environment.

## 5.2    INTERRUPTIONS AND WORK

In the last chapter I described different types of working spheres. In our data we looked at whether the types of interruptions might differ according to whether one is working in a working sphere that is for them central (for which they are accountable) or peripheral (for which they are not). Table 5.2 shows interruption type in relation to the source of the interruption. This is data of 35 people, using data of 11 additional participants compared to the data of 24 people reported in Mark et al. (2005). We might expect that most external interruptions would be in peripheral working spheres since one way that people become involved in peripheral work is that they are drawn into them to give advice. Colleagues may interrupt others to elicit expertise or opinions about their work. Table 5.2 shows that actually most external interruptions concern central working spheres (48.1%) whereas most internal interruptions are due to work that is personal, metawork, or unknown (58.7%). Metawork, as explained in the last chapter, refers to the high-level management of one's work, such as coordinating, checking activities, organizing email (as opposed to reading and answering it), organizing one's desktop, and catching up with teammates. Thus, when people self-interrupt, they are more likely to do so for either personal reasons or to organize their activities. People also spent significantly longer durations in working spheres that were self-interrupted compared to working spheres that were externally interrupted.

Table 5.2: Percent of internal/external interruptions according to the source of the interruption: central, peripheral, or "other" types of working spheres

| Interruption Source | External | Internal | % Interruption Source |
|---|---|---|---|
| **Central WS** | 48.1% | 35.7% | 41.2% |
| | (65.9%) | (34.1%) | |
| **Peripheral WS** | 22.8% | 5.6% | 15.2% |
| | (84.9%) | (15.1%) | |
| **Other WS (personal, metawork, unknown)** | 29.0% | 58.7% | 43.6% |
| | (37.6%) | (62.4%) | |
| **Percent external/internal interruptions** | (56.4%) | (43.6%) | 100% |

### 5.2.1    WORK ROLE

Work role makes a difference. There is a significant difference of internal/external interruptions and work role. We compared the average number of all types of interruptions *per person* by work role and found that developers had the highest average number of interruptions for their working spheres (59.7%), followed by analysts (49.3%), managers (39.7%), engineers (33.3%), and project team leaders (32.7%). Managers are more likely to experience external interruptions (59.2%) than internal interruptions (40.8%), whereas analysts and developers experience internal and external interruptions about equally. It makes sense that managers would experience more external interruptions since their jobs are more outward facing, as they supervise and continually deal with issues from others. Managers also generally perform delegation and coordination activities that could lead others who they are managing to interrupt. Managers have large social networks in the organization that increase the chances that a person in their social network will interrupt them. As managers generally interact in a wider circle of people than analysts and developers it should be expected that the chances are greater that they experience external interruptions compared to analysts and developers.

### 5.2.2  COMMUNICATIONS AND INTERRUPTIONS

Interruptions can affect workplace communications in interesting ways. Norman Su discovered that communication acts in the workplace occur in "chains of communication," which refers to how one communication act is followed by another (Su and Mark, 2008). People switch between solitary work and communications throughout the day. When people are interrupted from their solitary work either externally or internally, they tend to communicate in these "chains" which might involve switching to first be on a phone call, then to use email, and then to have a face-to-face interaction. One explanation for communication chains is that communication needs are stored up. When one is interrupted, then it is a chance to take care of communication needs that have accumulated.

When a person is externally interrupted for a communication (e.g., by receiving a phone call) then that person continues to do more subsequent communication acts than if one self-interrupts for a communication, such as to make a phone call. Communication chains triggered by external interruptions also had more different and novel media combinations compared to when they were triggered by self-interruptions. Perhaps external interruptions lead people to use a wider variety of communication media in order to accomplish the goals for that initial external interruption. We can well imagine that if one is interrupted by a colleague who needs some information, and if one does not know the answer, then one might contact other people to find the answer. Self-interruptions may involve less novel media combinations because perhaps they are triggered by a different motive such as by habit or when needing a break. Different goals for communication could well be associated with different kinds of interruptions.

## 5.3  INTERRUPTIONS AND THE ENVIRONMENT

### 5.3.1  COLLOCATION IN THE WORKPLACE

There are reasons to expect that collocated workers would experience fragmentation in their work to a greater extent than distributed workers. Informal interactions in the workplace have been described as spontaneous and opportunistic, providing rich sources of information that aid coordination (Kraut and Fish, 1993). On the other hand, distributed workers lack awareness of others' activities and interactions must be more planned and formal (Olson and Olson, 2000). We would also expect that collocated people might engage in more self-interruptions and task-switching to adapt to the activities of their colleagues. For example, overhearing a neighboring colleague speak on the phone about an application inconsistency might lead one to switch tasks to help review recent changes in that application.

The work environment could affect the influence of external interruptions, especially if one is in a closed office or open office environment. Considering that an open office environment affords people the opportunity to "talk through the walls" and quickly stop into others' cubicles, we hypothesized that collocated work would be interrupted more frequently. Using the same dataset of 35 people described above, we classified informants according to whether they were collocated or distributed from their teammates. Informants were considered *collocated* with their teammates when they were in a cubicle with at least one shared cubicle wall, i.e., where they could easily visit each other or talk through the cubicle walls or in a private office where they could talk with at least one teammate without leaving their office. Informants were considered distributed when they did not have at least one teammate sitting at an adjacent cubicle or in front of their office. Twenty-seven informants were co-located and eight were distributed from teammates as follows. There were 7 analysts, 8 developers, 6 managers, 2 engineers, 2 project leaders, and 2 managers who were collocated and 2 analysts, 3 project leaders, and 3 managers who were distributed.

Fragmentation of work concerns both working sphere length and interruptions. There was no significant difference in the length of time the collocated or distributed informants spent in their central working spheres. But we did find that collocated people overall experienced significantly more of their working sphere segments interrupted (57.0%) compared to distributed people (43.0%) (see Table 5.3). However, there was a significant difference with length of time in *peripheral* working spheres: the collocated informants showed a strong trend of spending longer lengths of time per working sphere segment that is peripheral to their main tasks. Also, collocated informants were involved in more peripheral working spheres each day on the average than distributed informants. In terms of interruptions, collocated people experience slightly more interruptions from peripheral work whereas distributed people experience more interruptions from personal, metawork, or other types of work. This result of collocation and peripheral work could be due to collocated people having more people around them who can interrupt them with issues not related to their central work. In other words, proximity could explain this result: it is easier for people to be spontaneously consulted by their neighboring colleagues for their expertise, and when they are, they tend to spend longer periods of time discussing the working sphere. Collocated people are thus drawn more into work that is peripheral for them.

As managers, analysts and developers were fairly evenly distributed over collocated/distributed settings, work role was not an explanation for these results. Although there were differences in amount of interruptions by work role, described above, we found no effect of work role in working sphere length, and no interaction of collocation and role.

Table 5.3: Percent of collocated/distributed interruptions according to the nature of the interruption. Data in parentheses are percentages within collocation

| Interruption Source | Collocated | Distributed | Total / (row avg) |
|---|---|---|---|
| **Central WS** | 58.4% | 41.6% | 100% |
| | (21.3%) | (20.1%) | (20.7%) |
| **Peripheral WS** | 67.2% | 32.8% | 100% |
| | (12.3%) | (8.0%) | (10.5%) |
| **Other WS\* (personal, metawork, unknown)** | 55.0% | 45.0% | 100% |
| | (66.4%) | (71.9%) | (68.8%) |
| **Column avg.** | 57.0%% | 43.0% | 100% |

Our observations can help to explain this. Awareness of when to interrupt collocated colleagues due to overhearing them was commonly observed and described during interviews. Informants listened to what their cubicle neighbors were doing and avoided interrupting when they were busy. When in doubt, they asked if they could interrupt. However, when they sensed that their colleagues were available, then they interrupted them. Sometimes people who did not need to be involved in a working sphere became involved through their collocation. The open office environment affords a culture of participation in solving problems even when people are not directly asked for advice. The informants described that they overheard problems that drew them in. For example, hearing a neighbor work on a system problem led them to check that part of the system that they were responsible for. In other cases, our informants described that they were on alert to offer their expertise to their colleagues, as one informant reported in Mark et al. (2005): "*I think my ears are always [alert] to listening to something because I find that my exposure….almost in every case I can lend something that some of the other people are not exposed to, you know they know their knowledge base, but once it passes that boundary they are kind of fuzzy on that.*"

### 5.3.2 ORGANIZATIONAL ENVIRONMENT

Perlow (1999) found that interruptions can be triggered by a work group or organizational culture. In other words, in some organizational cultures there is more of a willingness to readily interrupt others. The results of Dabbish et al. (2011) showed that organizational environments varied significantly in their self-interruption rates, and accounted for 13% of the variance in self-interruption rates. One reason to explain this difference is in how the informants interacted with their clients. In one group, an IT support branch of a financial analysis organization that *directly* dealt with clients, self-interruptions occurred at a significantly higher rate than participants in a second group, another IT branch in the same firm that dealt *indirectly* with clients or in a third group who worked in a high-tech medical device firm. This third group was more isolated from the real-time contact with the client, and more involved with the development, planning and quality assurance of the systems.

These differences found in organizational environments builds on the work of Perlow (1999) who found that the organizational environment affects external interruptions. Information-seeking norms are just one reason that self-interruption frequency may differ across organizations. The organizational environment may also be designed to be more or less distracting or conducive to self-interruption. Dabbish et al. (2011) also found that individuals seated in open office environments self-interrupted at a 64% significantly higher rate, which is similar to the results found when people were collocated with their teammates (Mark et al., 2005). In open office layouts all individuals can observe and overhear the interactions of all other individuals, which may create an environment conducive to self-interruptions (as well as external interruptions, as Mark et al. (2005) found).

### 5.3.3    TIME OF DAY

Hudson et al. (2002) discovered that managers prefer not to deal with interruptions at certain points in the day. Does time of day make a difference in multitasking? The data suggests it does. Although more interruptions occur in the morning (58%) compared to the afternoon (42%), this difference is not significant since there is so much variability. However, what is significantly different is the pattern of internal and external interruptions that occur throughout the day. Table 5.4 shows that the amount of external interruptions increases slightly from the morning (53.8%) to the afternoon (59.5%) while the amount of self interruptions decrease slightly over the day (from 46.2% to 40.5%). We also examined how time of day affects the length of time that people work in their central and peripheral working spheres. As reported in the last chapter, people work significantly shorter stretches in working spheres in the morning compared to the afternoon. Taken together, these results suggest that morning work has shorter segments and more self-interruptions; afternoon work has longer segments and more external interruptions. It is possible that work in the morning fuels information needs that trigger external interruptions later in the day.

| Table 5.4: External/internal interruptions in relation to work resumption | | | |
|---|---|---|---|
| | Type of Interruption | | Percentage Time of day |
| | External | Internal | |
| Morning | 55.6% (53.8%) | 61.2% (46.2%) | 58.0% |
| Afternoon | 44.4% (59.5%) | 38.8% (40.5%) | 42.0% |
| Percentage External/Internal | (56.2%) | (43.8%) | 100% |

## 5.4    INDIVIDUAL DIFFERENCES

Some people may be more susceptible to self-interruptions than others. Dabbish et al. (2011) found that individual differences in self-interruption accounted for 14% of the variance. Differences exist with gender and with personality traits.

### 5.4.1    GENDER

To discover whether there are gender differences with interruptions, we analyzed data from our sample of 6 female and 29 male informants, whose activities were measured to the second over 3 business days. There was no difference found with gender in the average length of time spent in a working sphere before switching. However, females worked in significantly more central and peripheral working spheres daily on the average than males. Moreover, there was a gender effect found for interruptions. Table 5.5 shows that female informants experienced fewer interruptions than males. Females were less likely to self-interrupt (32.5%) compared to their male colleagues (45.6%).

Females were significantly more likely to resume interrupted work (87.3%) than males (80.8%) on the same day. There was no significant difference between males and females in the length of time to resume interrupted work nor in the percent of working spheres self-resumed after an interruption. Based on this data, we might say that our female informants were more focused and more on task than our male informants. However, because this is a small sample of females, we urge further examination to explore gender differences with multitasking.

| Table 5.5: Percent of internal/external interruptions according to gender | | | |
|---|---|---|---|
| Gender | External | Internal | % for Female/Male |
| Female | 18.8% (67.5%) | 11.7% (32.5%) | 15.7% |
| Male | 81.2% (54.5%) | 88.3% (45.6%) | 84.3% |
| Percent type of interruption | (56.2%) | (43.8%) | 100% |

### 5.4.2    PERSONALITY TRAITS

Personality may influence how one responds to an interruption. The Big Five dimensions of personality have been widely employed as a measure of personality. The Big Five characterizes personality using five different traits: Agreeableness, Conscientiousness, Extraversion, Openness to Experience, and Extraversion. Mark et al. (2008) hypothesized that Openness to Experience and Conscientiousness could be related to how people handle interruptions. Openness to Experience refers to being open to change and variety and seeking diversity. Conscientiousness refers to the propensity for planning, the need for structure, and to seek high achievement. They expected that (a) the more open one is to new experiences (and thus better able to handle new tasks), and (b) the less need one has for personal structure (and thus is more flexible), the lower would be the disruption cost of an interruption. They felt that these measures would indicate if some can adapt quicker than others to a new situation (the interruption) and then more flexibly reorient back to the interrupted task.

Both "Openness to Experience" and "Conscientiousness" were found to be significant predictors of the time to complete an interrupted task. However, surprisingly, there was an inverse relationship: the higher one scored on Openness to Experience and also the higher one scored on Conscientiousness, the quicker it took to complete an interrupted task. We would expect the result of Openness to Experience: the more one is open to change and variety, the better able one might be to flexibly adapt to the environment. When one is interrupted, they could more easily and more quickly reorient and adapt back to the interrupted task. However, the result with Conscientiousness is very surprising. One explanation could be that the more structure people create for themselves, the more quickly they are able to handle interruptions and to get back on task. Perhaps people who score high on Conscientiousness have an internal plan or schedule to which they conform. Their work lives may be more structured and thus, if they are interrupted, they can retrieve this internal plan to more efficiently return to the task-at-hand.

## 5.5    CONSEQUENCES OF INTERRUPTIONS

### 5.5.1    RESUMPTION OF INTERRUPTED WORK

Resumption of interrupted work is also important to consider when examining interruptions. The characteristics associated with resuming interrupted tasks can provide clues on how much cognitive load people experience in a real work environment. Our observations reveal that from the informants' perspective, when they are interrupted they must reorient back to a particular context. The context is best defined at the level of working sphere. In other words, when people resume work, they refer to resuming the "TLX project." Therefore, we analyzed the resumption of interrupted work in terms of working spheres, as opposed to a finer-grained level of events. We only consider work that was interrupted and resumed on the same day in order to make a uniform comparison among all informants. Some people were observed on nonconsecutive days because they were out for a day, or because the weekend intervened. We also do not consider interrupted work during the last work hour, as there is less chance for it to be resumed that same day.

How often are tasks resumed? O'Connaill and Froehlich (1995) found that 41% of the time an interrupted task was not resumed right away. However, O'Connaill and Froehlich did not measure whether an interrupted task was returned to at some point later in the day. We did examine the extent to which interrupted tasks are resumed at a point later in the day to find out how much intervening work existed on average. We found that 40% of all working spheres were interrupted on average throughout the day. However, the good news is that most working spheres that were interrupted were resumed on the same day (81.9%). What type of work was most likely to be resumed? Not surprisingly, people's interrupted central working spheres were about twice as likely to be resumed on the same day (82.0%) compared to people's interrupted peripheral working spheres (43.8%). We would expect this since people are accountable for their central working spheres and we would expect more attention would be directed to resuming work in them as soon as possible.

It might be expected that the longer one works in a working sphere, the faster one might resume work in it when it is interrupted, following the Zeigarnik effect, which describes that interrupted tasks produce a tension (Greist-Bousquet and Schiffman, 1992). People strive to reduce the tension by resuming an unfinished task and the Zeigarnik effect predicts that the closer one is to finishing a task, the more tension is created. However, we found that the length of time that one worked in a working sphere before being interrupted bore no relation to whether the work was resumed later that day or not.

External and internal interruptions may affect whether and how fast work is resumed. Table 5.6 shows how external and self-interruptions relate to the resumption of work. There is a trend that externally interrupted working spheres were more likely to be resumed on the same day than internally interrupted working spheres. Externally interrupted working spheres are also resumed on the average in a shorter time than internally interrupted working spheres. One reason for these results could be that when people self-interrupt, they are doing so for a break or to let a problem incubate. It may take more time then, compared to an external interruption that brings people away from their task. It could also be related to the Zeigarnik effect discussed earlier. Perhaps external interruptions create more tension for people to return to interrupted tasks compared to self-interruptions, as external interruptions are not under people's control. Self-interruptions however, might be used for taking a break, and people may feel less pressure to return quickly to the task.

Table 5.6: External/internal interruptions in relation to whether work was resumed on the same day

|  | Type of Interruption | | |
|  | External | Internal | |
| --- | --- | --- | --- |
| Resumed | 85.9% (57.1%) | 82.8% (42.9%) | 84.5% |
| Not resumed | 14.1% (51.3%) | 17.2% (48.7%) | 15.5% |
| Total | (56.2%) | (43.8%) | 100% |

How long does it take people to resume a task when it is interrupted? Unfortunately, we found that people do not return to their interrupted working sphere right away. When people did resume work on the same day, it took an average length of time of 23 min and 15 s to return to their interrupted work. They worked in an average of 1.92 other working spheres before resuming the interrupted task. We can unpack this figure of roughly two intervening working spheres as follows. People's attention was directed to multiple other topics before resuming work. A general pattern is that one is interrupted, switches to another working sphere, then switches again to a second working sphere, and then returns back to the original interrupted working sphere. Thus, one experiences multiple cognitive shifts before returning back to the original task. This general pattern suggests that interruptions are nested.

Thus, people's attention was directed to multiple other topics before resuming work. This was reported by informants as being very detrimental for their work. In some cases, from the observations, the physical or desktop environment was restructured, which makes it more difficult to rely on cues to reorient to an interrupted task. For example, a paper laid on top of a pile is a signal that this is work to be resumed. If that paper becomes covered then this cue is less obvious. A blinking cursor at the end of the last typed word can enable one to immediately reorient to that place in the document, whereas if other windows have been opened, it can be hard to remember even which document had been worked on.

There can be different mechanisms by which people can resume work based on observations. Sometimes people resumed interrupted working spheres on their own. Other times interrupted working spheres were brought to the attention of the informant, for example through phone calls, or by a manager or colleague who asks about the status of a project. We examined the differences between the external and internal resumption of interrupted work.

We coded the data into two types of work resumption: externally-initiated resumption, where an external action led people to resume work: phone calls, people showing up in the cubicle, or people in adjacent cubicles talking to them "through the wall," and self-initiated resumption where no evidence was observed that another person was associated with the resumption of work. Of interrupted work that was resumed on the same day, only a small proportion was due to externally initiated resumptions (9.9%) compared to work that was resumed by one's self (90.1%). The amount of time before working spheres were externally resumed was significantly longer than working spheres that were self-resumed. Thus, people are more likely to resume work on their own and to do it faster than when interactions with others lead them to do it.

Collocation also affects the resumption of work. A higher proportion of interrupted working spheres are resumed on the same day when people are distributed (82.1%) compared to when people are collocated (74.3%). Collocated workers showed a trend to resume work more due to externally initiated resumption (11.2%) compared to distributed workers (7.9%). The effects of proximity to colleagues can therefore not only lead to more interruptions but also can serve to help people resume interrupted work.

## 5.5.2   INTERRUPTIONS AND CONTEXT

Mark et al. (2008) measured the *disruption cost* of interruptions. One type of disruption cost is the additional time to reorient back to an interrupted task after the interruption is handled. Previous studies introduce conflicting notions as to whether the interruption context is related to a disruption cost (Adamczyk and Bailey, 2004; Czerwinski et al., 2004; Hudson et al., 2002; Mark et al., 2005). For example, Czerwinski et al. (2000) found that interruptions that were consistent with the task-at-hand facilitated the task. One might be working on a paper and be interrupted by a completely different topic, such as a question about a budget. If an interruption has a different context than the current task at-hand, this could introduce a disruption cost as it involves a cognitive shift of context to attend to the interruption, and then one must reorient back to attend to the interrupted task. On the other hand, one might be interrupted by a question that concerns the same context as the paper one is working on. This might be beneficial but if the context of the interruption and primary task are similar, this could lead to interference with the primary task (cf. Gillie and Broadbent, 1989) and in this way may introduce a disruption cost. A third possibility is that the interruption context may not matter. Perhaps any discontinuity in the task creates a disruption cost for work.

To test whether the context of an interruption affects the disruption cost, Mark et al. (2008) simulated an office environment in the laboratory. Forty-eight participants were given an email task to perform, common in information work. No interruptions were given in the baseline condition. In the "same context" interruption condition, participants were interrupted by questions concerning the current task context. In the "different context" interruption condition, participants were interrupted by questions about a different topic not related to the context of the task-at-hand. These interruptions were on random topics, designed to simulate the types of interruptions one might expect in real office work. Interruptions were also given in one of two mediums: by telephone or by instant message. Participants were instructed to attend to interruptions immediately, i.e., to pick up the telephone or attend to the IM window.

The total time that it took to perform the task was compared in all the conditions. The time to perform the task was computed as the total time to perform the task minus the time spent on interruptions. If the time to perform the task was higher with an interruption, then this would indicate that extra time was needed to perform the task after an interruption. Surprisingly, participants took the longest time in the baseline condition to perform the task and there was no significant difference between the two interruption contexts nor did the media used to convey the interruption make a difference. It was then examined whether the reason that it took longer to do the task in the uninterrupted condition is because people wrote more. Indeed, it was found that email messages were longest in the baseline condition, with no interruptions.

Were people less accurate when interrupted? What about politeness? Were people who were interrupted less polite in their email replies? Errors were measured as spelling errors, typos or others (e.g., misspelled names) and accuracy of the responses were checked. A politeness metric was computed by assigning points for the use of standard greeting/closing phrases and politeness words. There were no differences in politeness of messages nor in accuracy or errors.

The results showed that *any* interruption introduces a change in work pattern and is not related to context per se. The results differed from Gillie and Broadbent (1989) who found similarity of cognitive processes of interruptions to a task were disruptive. Interruptions that share a context with the main task may be *perceived* as being beneficial but the actual disruption cost, when measured in time, is the same as when interruptions relate to a different context than the main task.

### 5.5.3    INTERRUPTIONS AND STRESS

In the experimental study of Mark et al. (2008), it was then explored whether interruptions led to stress. Stress can be a cost of disruption in work. Using the NASA mental workload measures (Hart and Staveland, 1988) across interruption type, stress was found to be highest for both interruption conditions (same and different contexts) compared to the baseline condition. Level of frustration, time pressure, and amount of effort were reported highest in both interruption conditions compared to the baseline. Perceived workload was highest for the "different context" interruption condition.

It was next examined whether stress might be due to interrupted work taking longer to accomplish. Surprisingly, the results showed that interrupted work is performed faster. Perhaps when people are constantly interrupted, they develop a mode of working faster (and writing less) to compensate for the time they know they will lose by being interrupted. People have a finite amount of time in the workday. If they know they are working in an environment where they expect interruptions, than they may adjust their pace of work to accommodate interruptions.

Yet, working faster with interruptions has its cost: people in the interrupted conditions experienced a higher workload, more stress, higher frustration, more time pressure, and effort. So interrupted work may be done faster, but at a price. A certain amount of interruptions may be tolerable because people can compensate with a higher working speed. However, in this laboratory study, after only 20 min of interrupted performance, people reported significantly higher stress, frustration, workload, effort, and pressure. Over an entire workday we might expect the results to be even stronger. However, in a real-world context, people may take breaks to relieve themselves of stress. These results confirm experimentally the anecdotal reports of informants in field studies who describe high stress when interrupted in real work situations (Mark et al., 2005).

### 5.5.4    CONTROL OF INTERRUPTIONS

Interruptions during the course of the workday might be of the same context as the current task at-hand or they might relate to completely other topics. Earlier, I discussed that interruptions could be beneficial or disruptive. It could be that interruptions that relate to the current task-at-hand could be beneficial. They could provide needed information or help one think about the task in a different way. Interruptions that do not relate to the task-at-hand could be disruptive as they cause one to make a cognitive shift to deal with a different topic.

If people are given control over when they can be interrupted, for example to help inform the task at-hand, interruptions should be perceived as beneficial. This idea was tested by Yuzawa and Mark (2010) with a prototype called the Japanese Garden which allowed users to control when they could be interrupted, by whom, and on what topic. The prototype was designed with a tangible interface modeled after a Japanese Garden. Using camera color recognition, the users could place colored artifacts representing their different working spheres in particular positions to indicate their availability for interruption (Figure 5.1). The results showed that the use of the prototype system reduced the amount of coordination and resulted in fewer interruptions for the interruptee. In other words, being able to control interruptions to gear them to one's current work context showed benefits.

Figure 5.1: Prototype of the Japanese Garden, a tangible interface to manage interruptions.

## 5.6    SUMMARY AND DISCUSSION: THE NATURE OF INTERRUPTIONS WITH DIGITAL MEDIA

This chapter discussed a range of findings related to interruptions in a real-world context. To summarize, the main results related to interruptions are shown in Table 5.7.

Whereas most studies focus on external interruptions, in fact interruptions can be externally or internally initiated. Perhaps one of the most interesting findings of this chapter is that people are nearly as likely to self-interrupt as to be interrupted by others. Why would people self-interrupt? It is possible that people might have a need or perhaps may even be conditioned to take breaks. If an external interruption does not occur for some time, then perhaps people simply interrupt themselves.

Table 5.7: Summary of factors that are associated with interruptions

| Factor | Result |
| --- | --- |
| **Types of Interruptions** | |
| External (EXT) vs. Internal (INT) interruptions | Nearly the same frequency |
| Relationship of EXT with INT | EXT predict INT in next hour |
| **Interruptions and work** | |
| Central vs. Peripheral working spheres (WS) | More EXT are to central WS; More INT are for personal, metawork activities |
| Work role | Managers experience more EXT |
| Communication | EXT lead to more communication acts in a row |
| **Workplace environment** | |
| Collocation | Collocated people had more interruptions, from peripheral work |
| Organizational environment | Differences in self-interruption rates |
| Time of day | EXT increases slightly over the day INT decreases slightly over the day |
| **Individual characteristics** | |
| Gender | Females less likely to have INT; resume more interrupted work the same day |
| Personality | Higher scores on Openness to Experience, Conscientiousness, the quicker to complete an interrupted task |
| **Consequences of interruptions** | |
| Resumption of work | Avg. of 23 min, 15 s. to resume an interrupted task; Avg. of 1.92 intervening WS |
| Context | Interruptions induce a cost, independent of context |
| Stress | Interruptions cause stress |
| Control | Controlling interruptions reduced coordination; fewer interruptions |

We expect that polychronics (those who prefer switching between tasks) should have higher levels of self-interruption, irrespective of the task (Bluedorn et al., 1992). Self-interruptions could be due to individual differences in the ability to focus. Work on self-reported multitasking behavior and attention suggests that as individuals' attentional capacity is different, this could influence people's tendency to self-interrupt (Ophir et al., 2009). Another reason to explain self-interruptions could be due to being conditioned to interrupt based on experiencing external interruptions. Dabbish et al. (2011) found that external interruptions in the previous hour predicted self-interruptions in the subsequent hour. If one is used to experiencing external interruptions, and then they wane, then perhaps one begins to self-interrupt simply to keep up the rhythm of interruptions. However, the role of external interruptions explain a smaller amount of variance relative to individual differences and organizational factors.

When one is interrupted on a task, it takes on average over 23 min to resume work back on that interrupted task. Meanwhile, people work on average in nearly two other working spheres before resuming the interrupted task. Previous work on interruptions did not capture the intervening activity that occurred before a task is resumed. Such intervening activity uses cognitive resources and this makes the task of reorienting back to an interrupted task that much harder.

There is a gender effect with interruptions: females self-interrupt less than their male counterparts and resume interrupted work faster. One caveat is that there were only six females in the sample. However, there was a large amount of data generated for each person (three days, activities measured to the second). It is important to consider that the females in the sample were professionals in non-traditional work roles for women. It warrants further examination to understand why a gender difference exists with interruptions.

Proximity to others affects interruptions. Being collocated draws people more into their colleagues' work, and this work is often peripheral for the person drawn in. But proximity to others also appears to influence people in resuming interrupted work, perhaps through overhearing words that trigger reminders. These results have implications for the design of open office environments which offer both costs and benefits.

The laboratory results showing that interruptions can cause stress, combined with the result that people perform intervening work before resuming a task, together suggest that in a real-world context, interruptions could create a high amount of stress. There is a cognitive load of having to keep the states of interrupted tasks in mind, and also having to reorient back to interrupted tasks. Further, intervening tasks also involve mental resources and can interfere with the ability to reorient back to an interrupted task.

The study showing a relationship of personality traits and interruptions by Mark et al. (2008) was done in a laboratory where interruptions were induced. The advantage of a laboratory study is that it enables the testing of causality; the disadvantage is that it cannot simulate many aspects of real-world environments. It would be interesting for further research to examine whether Big Five traits are related to people's propensity to self-interrupt and also to how they respond to external interruptions, especially in a real-world context. For example, we might expect that people who score high in Extroversion also experience more external interruptions, since they more readily interact with others. Some support for this idea is found from the work of Mark and Ganzach (2014d) who discovered that people who score high on Extraversion also engage in more online communication. Ryan and Xenos (2011) also found that Facebook users scored high on Extraversion. We might expect then that Facebook use is associated with self-interruptions, so it may be possible that Extraverts also self-interrupt more. This is rich material for further research. In the next chapter we will address a main source of interruptions: email.

# CHAPTER 6

# Email

A discussion on multitasking in an *in situ* environment would not be complete without including email. The popular press keeps ridiculing our obsession with email. A few years ago, a *New York Times* article drew an analogy between zombies and emails: the zombies keep coming even though you keep killing them, and emails keep coming even though you keep deleting them (Klosterman, 2010). The popular cartoon Oatmeal characterizes how the "email monster" plagues us (theoatmeal. com/comics/email_monster). Over the years, from interviews and anecdotal reports, our informants who have been observed while performing information work *in situ* claim the main reason for their self-interruptions is from checking email. In this chapter I will discuss how email is a significant contributor to multitasking in a digital media environment.

Recently, I received an email message from a friend who had not responded to an email that I had sent about a week prior. I resent the email and asked him if he had received it. His reply at 6:52 p.m. on that same day was:

> Oh darn it. No, I didn't get you earlier email, don't know why. But even if I had I couldn't have done anything about it. I've been terribly busy, gone part of the time myself, back this weekend for a party for my wife's daughter who's about to have a baby.....

But then I received a second message at 6:56 p.m.:

> PS. Now I'm really embarrassed. Your Dec 1 email *did* make it into my inbox. I was gone and when I returned to my computer I simply overlooked it among the piles of junkmail I don't seem to be able to escape. Sorry. But as I said, I couldn't have done anything about it anyway; I could, however have let you know that, and I apologize for not doing so.

How often do we all receive messages and then find out later (sometimes months later) that we never replied to them? We blame the flood of emails that invade our inbox or that the email gets sent to our junk folder (without our intention). I cannot count the times that I missed important emails that clearly and legitimately landed in my inbox. What is perhaps even worse is that, more than I like to think about, I opened a message, fully planning to respond to it later that day, and then totally forgot about it, remembering weeks or months later. Perhaps it is best that I do not even know about the messages I missed.

Why is it that people who love to communicate with others are so disturbed by email? Sherry Turkle writes that *"we don't do email, our email does us"* (Turkle, 2010). Similarly, Barley et al. (2011) found that 45% of participants in their study associated email with a loss of control. On the other hand, Mazmanian et al. (2013) found that email use on mobile devices afforded information workers control of their activities, at least for short periods. There could, however, be individual differences in how people feel about email. Huang and Lin (2014) found that information workers who scored higher in self-efficacy and who had better time management skills, felt more in control of their email use. In fact, this was independent of the volume of email received. However, many people do not possess such a combination of self-efficacy and time management skills. What is it about email in particular that leads people to not feel in control of it?

As with any communication application, there is not just a one-sided view. Email certainly provides benefits in the workplace. Whittaker and Sidner (1996) pointed out that email, which had been originally designed as a communication medium, has expanded vastly in its utility. Email is a multi-functional tool. It is used as a to-do list and personal information management tool (Belotti et al., 2005), as a mechanism to foster coordination and collaboration among colleagues, and as a source for assigning and delegating tasks (Whittaker andSidner, 1996), for task management, archiving information, and as a clearinghouse for personal contacts (Whittaker et al., 2006). It has been found to speed up communication and benefit work performance (Mano and Mesch, 2010). In a review of email research, Ducheneut and Watts (2011) classified email research approaches into three categories: considering email as a filing cabinet, as a production facility for organizational communication, and as a communication genre. Email, without question, affords a variety of uses for managing information work. So why then, despite all the benefits and varied uses that email affords, do people complain about it? Does email actually cause a feeling of overload or is it just a myth? Does email contribute significantly to multitasking?

## 6.1    EMAIL OVERLOAD

Overload of information refers to when the amount of information that needs to be attended to exceeds a person's capacity to process that information (Schultze and Vandenbosch, 1998). Farhoomand and Drury (2002) identified two reasons that contribute to feeling overloaded from information: when there is too much information to manage, and when people lack the time to deal with the information. Both of these reasons could apply to email. Managing the sheer volume of email is one factor that could contribute to a perception of overload (Wacjman and Rose, 2011). It is not just the amount of email already in one's inbox, but that email keeps arriving continually. If email keeps landing and piling up in the inbox, this can contribute to a feeling of being overwhelmed especially if one feels they need to attend to that email. Like the zombies, the email keeps coming irrespective of our actions. Some support for the idea of incoming email as overload is found in a study by Dabbish et al. (2005): messages that are perceived to be important and require a lot of work to answer tended to be left in the inbox for later. The emails in the inbox remain as pending tasks: they are always lurking in the background. The amount of time spent managing email could also contribute to feeling overloaded with email: the more time people spend dealing with email, the more overloaded people feel (Barley et al., 2011). There is an opportunity cost with email; managing email takes time away from other workplace tasks. The time expended in doing email could create time pressure to complete other tasks, leading to stress.

Poor email management strategies also play a role in feeling overloaded (Dabbish and Kraut, 2006). Keeping track of separate email threads can also add to email strain (Bellotti et al., 2005). Meeting the demands of the sender can also add to a sense of feeling overwhelmed when using email (Renaud et al., 2006). This could especially be true if the sender is higher up in the organizational hierarchy. Thus, it may not be just the work involved in answering queries but it is a far larger endeavor of using email in work. Yet another reason for perceived overload has been attributed to the poor design of email clients that are not geared to facilitate organization and retrieval of emails (Szotek, 2010). This puts a burden on the user to find the relevant email. There certainly are plenty of reasons why email can lead people to feel overloaded with information.

Last, although the use of mobile devices may offer users a sense of control as to when and where they can access email, an alternative perspective proposes that mobile devices break down work-life boundaries (Middleton and Cukler, 2006). When boundaries of work and personal life become indistinguishable, then work life (especially if driven by email) is hard to turn off. This can lead to feeling overloaded due to the extended workday.

Feeling overloaded is associated with stress. We would therefore also expect email use to be associated with stress. Based on self-reports, studies suggest indeed that it is (Barley et al., 2011; Dabbish and Kraut, 2006; Renaud et al., 2006; Mano and Mesch, 2010; Kushlev and Dunn, 2015). Self-reports of stress, however, can be biased, especially if participants feel that reporting stress is the appropriate response for email usage (cf. Donaldson and Grant-Vallone, 2002). In an experimental study comprised of mostly students, it was found that checking email less frequently was associated with lower self-reported stress (Kushlev and Dunn, 2015). However, in this study, in the baseline condition the participants were specifically instructed to check their email as frequently as they could. This instruction could have encouraged people to check more than they ordinarily do, leading to an inflated difference of reported stress compared to the condition with restricted email checking.

In the last two chapters I discussed the extent to which people multitask and are interrupted. Much switching between computer screens concerns looking at email. Another perspective of how email contributes to overload is that with its use, people are constantly shifting activities. At a finer-grained level, people are switching among the operations of checking, composing, reading and writing email, and doing other work. Examining this at a more course-grained level of working spheres, people are switching between different working spheres as emails lead them to engage in different tasks. Thus, managing email contributes to the fragmentation of work.

## 6.2    EMAIL AND MULTITASKING

Evidence suggests that people do switch between email and other work frequently. Checking email can be an interruption in the flow of work. Although estimates do vary, they do tell a consistent story: people check their email inbox quite a bit over the course of a day. Over a decade ago, Jackson et al. (2003) found that 70% of emails were attended to within six seconds of arriving. Email may not be so distracting if workers quickly returned to their interrupted task; however, these researchers found that it took an average of 64 s to resume an interrupted task. Contrasting this result with the earlier result that showed it took people 10 1/2 min to resume a working sphere, it could be that Jackson et al. (2003) were measuring the recovery from email interruption at a finer-grained level of granularity. Renaud et al. (2006) logged 6 users and found that they switched to email about 36 times an hour, which is far higher than the estimate of Jackson et al. (2003). A more recent estimate, however, using logging techniques with a larger sample of 32 people over one week, found that people averaged checking email about 74 times a day, which is roughly about 11 times per hour (Mark et al., 2015). These varying estimates could be due to the different cultures examined (the U.K. vs. North America), the type of job role, the year of the study, and the type of organization. Despite the differences in estimates, there is one common theme: email interrupts the flow of work.

How much time does email actually demand in a workday? Studies show with consistency that people spend a large portion of their time in the workplace on email. The estimates vary, however. Renaud et al. (2010) found that 84% of people in a survey reported that they kept their email clients open in the background and 64% used notifications all or part of the time. Wacjman and Rose (2011) found that, on average, information workers engage in more mediated communication each day than face-to-face communication, of which email is the most common. In a self-report diary study, Czerwinski et al. (2004) found that 23% of the tasks that people reported doing in the workday was email. In 2006, using a logging technique, information workers were found to average receiving 87 emails daily (Fisher et al., 2006). Mark et al. (2015) found that information workers spent a total daily average duration of 34 min, 31 s dealing with email, but when the entire use of the personal information manager Outlook is considered as well (i.e., checking the inbox, but also the calendar), then the average duration shoots up to 118 min daily.

Fisher et al. (2006) found that the size of information workers' email archives grew tenfold in a ten-year period, with a mean of over 28,000 items. Also considering spam, users repeatedly claim that there are too many email messages to keep up with (Whittaker and Sidner, 1996; Bellotti et al., 2003; Dabbish and Kraut, 2006). Associated with this issue is the lack of time needed to manage the email. As more email messages pile up, more time is needed to respond to them. These widely varying estimates could be due to the different methodologies used to assess the duration of time spent on email. Self-reports can overestimate email usage; people are found to be poor estimates of the length of time they use information technology (Collopy, 1996).

One of the difficulties in assessing and comparing email use is that it has been studied with various methods. Email usage has been observed *in situ* (Bellotti et al., 2005; Renaud et al., 2006), with diaries (Czerwinski et al., 2004), perspectives on its use have been gained through surveys (Dabbish and Kraut, 2006; Mano and Mesch, 2010) and the objective time spent in email has been captured through logging techniques (Jackson et al., 2003). Continuing the theme of observing email *in situ*, in the rest of this chapter I report results from both objective and user perspectives. I will present results on email usage and how it impacts stress, focus, and behavior. These results may help shed light on the extent to which email fragments work and why email is perceived to be so bothersome.

## 6.3    CUTTING OFF EMAIL: A STUDY

Studies of email use thus suggest a pattern that managing email is associated with a feeling of being overwhelmed, overloaded, stressed, and with a loss of control. However, what is the role of email and multitasking? As explained in earlier chapters, I refer to multitasking as switching between different tasks that are interleaved. Does email lead people to interleave tasks? With email, do people focus less on other work? Do they self-interrupt to check messages that arrived in the inbox? If so, then email could lead work to become more fragmented. Is it possible to create an environment where people can become more focused? What if people worked without email? Would their work be less fragmented and would they be more engaged in work? Unfortunately, there have not been detailed logging studies to examine the switching of attention before email came into widespread usage in organizations.

In 2011, along with Stephen Voida, we examined the effect of cutting off email with people in an organization (Mark et al., 2012). There were several reasons that motivated this study. Above all, we were interested to understand the effects that email has on work, on colleagues, and on people's stress levels. By removing email from people's work lives, it enabled us to take an inverse perspective from the previous studies that were conducted examining email use; instead we could ask: how do people and the environment change without email?

Our reasoning for cutting off email was threefold. First, it enabled us to understand whether it is possible to create an environment in which people can focus more closely on their tasks. Since people self-interrupt to check email often (e.g., Jackson et al., 2003), if email were not available would people spend a longer duration of focus on their work? In other words, would work become less fragmented? Second, it enabled us to measure how much stress was associated with email use. We could compare a baseline measure (with email use) with an intervention where email was cut off. Last, it provided participants with a different experience and perspective about email use so that they could reflect more deeply about the effects of email.

It took over six years to find an organization that was willing to let some of its employees cut off email for this study. A willing organization was finally found—a large scientific research and development organization. The organization was interested to participate to learn more about how their employees were affected by email. The senior managers felt that email overload was a real problem in the organization. Thirteen people (6 females, 7 males) agreed to cut off their email for one workweek. The participants had a high degree of job autonomy.

Table 6.1: Means and SDs of the observed durations (in seconds) of types of activities, excluding personal breaks

| Activity Type | Baseline | | No Email | |
|---|---|---|---|---|
| | Mean | SD | Mean | SD |
| Out of office* (work-related) | 412.32 | 938.14 | 1195.24 | 2048.88 |
| Computing tasks | 52.47 | 90.52 | 50.32 | 82.81 |
| Physical tasks (e.g., reading, jotting notes) | 41.06 | 75.55 | 56.55 | 69.86 |
| Communication in the office (excl. email) | 84.82 | 256.94 | 60.15 | 103.68 |
| Email (new/filed) | 40.65 | 60.71 | 36.94 | 64.85 |
| Metawork* | 21.41 | 28.04 | 29.14 | 41.76 |
| Other tasks | 56.12 | 205.58 | 31.33 | 54.50 |
| **Overall** | **74.81** | **375.37** | **102.85** | **510.81** |

* = sig. difference between Baseline and No Email at $p < .05$

For three days each participant had their computer activity logged for a baseline measure. Then, participants had their email cut off for five days, a full workweek. Participants were also shadowed using the same observational approach described in the earlier chapters where the observer sat behind the person or followed them around and recorded and timed their activities to the second using a stop watch. To directly measure how email might affect stress, participants wore heart rate monitors on a chest strap full time while at work. Heart rate variability is widely used as an indicator of mental stress (see Acharya et al., 2006 for a review). Counter-intuitively, the lower the HRV, the higher the level of stress for an individual. The reason is that the body responds to stressful circumstances by regulating itself. When people are more relaxed, HRV is higher, as the body is not regulating itself and heart rate fluctuates more. People are more responsive to stimuli and even a small stimulus can drive up the heart rate.

While cut off from email, participants stayed connected with colleagues through informal interaction, telephone calls, and by having team members notify them (mostly face-to-face) of critical emails sent to the entire work group. In the baseline condition, participants regularly checked email.

The email cut off condition had an unexpected effect. By the fifth day of email cutoff, participants rarely checked their email.

Table 6.1 shows that, based on the observational data, two main differences were found when email was cut off. First, people spent significantly more time in out-of-office work-related activities when cut off from email compared to when they used email. Second, people spent significantly longer doing metawork, i.e., managing their work through the use of calendars or organizing their work through various means.

Table 6.2 shows, for each participant, durations (in seconds) that application and document windows were recorded as active, and the frequency of window switches (in switches per hour). For all but one participant, the mean window duration was longer during the No Email condition compared to Baseline. The data show that participants spent significantly longer durations on any document or application when email was cut off compared to the baseline. In terms of the frequency of window switches, all participants had a lower average frequency of window switches when email was cut off compared to baseline. Thus, participants in the No Email condition switched their windows significantly less often than in the Baseline condition. Switching windows is a proxy for switching attention and switching activities. Together, these results reveal that without email, people did switch their attention less frequently with a longer task focus. In other words, the results show that email usage leads to more work fragmentation.

Table 6.2: Mean and SD of window duration (in seconds) and frequency of window switches (switches/hour in which data were collected) for participants

| Baseline | | | | No Email | | | |
|---|---|---|---|---|---|---|---|
| Duration | | Frequency | | Duration | | Frequency | |
| Mean | SD | Mean | SD | Mean | SD | Mean | SD |
| 75.5 | 394.3 | 37.1 | 31.4 | 131.9 | 568.1 | 18.2 | 23.5 |

## 6.4    EMAIL AND STRESS

Table 6.3 shows measures averaged for each condition over all the days that data were collected. The data revealed that people in the baseline condition had lower heart rate variability (i.e., higher stress) than when email was cut off. A comparison of the heart rate variability of all baseline data with all the data during the email cutoff shows this difference to be highly significant. These results indicate that participants experienced less stress when their email was cut off than in the baseline condition when they used email as they did normally.

It is difficult to disentangle the different sources of stress in the workplace, so we can only speculate as to whether it is the volume of email, social expectations and organizational conventions associated with email, or email as a channel for delegating work that led to the increase in stress. The fact that stress levels changed in only five days without email suggests that short "vacations" from email may be sufficient to reduce stress in the workplace. In fact, such brief email vacations could be good for health. If workplace stress is detrimental to health, as some research suggests (Hewlett and Luce, 2006), then the results may even suggest that email could contribute to workplace health problems by raising stress levels. The fact that being without email reduced stress and that people moved around the workplace more supports the idea that reducing the use of email could even be good for health. This is a topic for further research.

Table 6.3: Mean and SD of heart rate monitor data for each condition. Note that the higher the standard deviation, the lower is the stress

| Baseline | | No Email | |
| --- | --- | --- | --- |
| Mean | SD | Mean | SD |
| 77.03 | 16.173 | 80.39 | 18.36 |

## 6.5    PERSPECTIVES ON CUTTING OFF EMAIL

How did the informants themselves feel when their email was cut off for five days? In-depth interviews after the email cut off study was finished provided some insight. When email was cut off, it gave the participants a unique opportunity to reflect on how email affects them in work and personal life. Consistent with the objective logged computer activity, nearly all the participants reported that when email was cut off, they were able to focus more intently on their work. They explained that they could spend more time on critical work and they could work a longer chunk of time on a single project.

Email was perceived as a burden due to the sheer volume of email received. The informants commonly reported not being able to keep up with their email. They referred to important emails that get lost in the flood of incoming messages. Despite the findings by Huang and Lin (2014) that suggested that some personality types can exhibit self-control with email, none of our participants reported being able to do this. The participants admitted that they lacked self-control to prevent themselves from checking email continually, which for some, translated into a lack of agency that applied more broadly across their work. One person expressed this feeling aptly:

*I let the sound of the bell and the pop-ups rule my life.*

One possibility that contributed to why stress was reduced without email was that when email was cut off, the participants interacted more with their colleagues in face-to-face interactions. Although they could use the telephone, some even walked to other buildings on the campus. The observational data corroborate this. As shown in Table 6.1, the participants spent a significantly longer time out of their office (in work related activities) when email was cut off. On the whole, the informants reported that they enjoyed their social life at work with their colleagues more when email was cut off. Some participants reflected that the use of email hindered their work relationships, as one person described:

> …*Email can be a superficial blanket that distances you from real relationships where you're really working together.*

Yet, on the other hand, email serves to connect people to others. A reason why people continually check email that is email connects them to a web of colleagues, and to the organization. About half the informants described being without email access as a general sense of isolation. One participant explained:

> *Yes—hands down—it isolates you as the one person who's not "plugged in."*

This comments highlights the notion that any individual who wants to cut off email or slow down their response to email would be penalized. They would be perceived as "out of the loop" in organizational matters.

Cutting off email may affect not only the individual but also colleagues; it can affect their ability to seek information from that individual. Interestingly, the colleagues in the participants' work groups did not report detrimental effects when their colleagues were off email. The participants' closest colleagues reported that their satisfaction, productivity, and stress levels were not affected but they did report that it was harder to get information from their colleague (which was expected).

## 6.5.1 SOCIAL NORMS AND EMAIL USE

The interviews revealed social norms associated with emails. The informants commonly expressed that there is a norm or expectation that the email recipient will respond to an email quickly. For example, one informant comes into work two hours later than her colleagues. She described how her colleagues, who arrived at work and sent out emails two hours prior, expect an answer to their emails as soon as she arrives. Because her schedule is different than her colleagues, she cannot respond to all her emails as rapidly as her colleagues expect her to. The social norm of rapid response to an email works against this person whose schedule is not in synch with her colleagues.

Another social norm is that it is acceptable for email to be used as a channel for delegating tasks to others. One person, who had their email cut off, described how his supervisor sends him tasks via email that are expected to be done immediately. As a lab scientist, this interferes with his ability to set up and run experiments without interruption. When his email was cut off, the task requests suddenly stopped even though the supervisor could have called him on the phone or walked down the hall to delegate the task to him face-to-face. This experience led him to believe that the tasks he had been receiving by email were either not important or that the senders had taken initiative to find the information themselves when he was off email. This suggests that email is an acceptable means (at least for managers) for delegating work.

## 6.6    EMAIL, MOOD, AND FOCUSED ATTENTION

How does email affect mood? In an *in situ* study of digital media use, email use was found to be associated with negative emotion (Mark et al., 2014a). Thirty-two information workers were tracked over a full workweek and were asked to rate their mood, using an experience sampling methodology. In experience sampling, participants received probes on their computer screen and were asked to rate their mood "right now." The mood that was reported was then correlated with the computer activity that people had just performed before the probe came up. The results showed a significant positive correlation between negative mood and the amount of email use in the 5-min window before the probe appeared. The more email that people dealt with, the more negative they reported their mood to be. Simply put, doing email puts people in a bad mood.

One reason that might explain why email puts people in a bad mood could be due to the effort needed to use email. In the same study of 32 information workers described above, participants also reported how focused they were in the activity they were just doing. In a further analysis, the same authors found a correlation between doing email and being focused (Mark et al., 2014b). Thus, doing email involves focus.

It may be that if people are focused then they are in a "preparatory state" for doing email. In other words, if people are already focused, then perhaps it is less effort to get into a focused state in order to do email. Why not do email if you are already prepared for it? This was indeed found. Mark et al. (2015) discovered that when people are already in a focused attentional state, then they subsequently spend a significantly longer time doing email compared to when they are not focused.

Together, these results about email, mood, and attentional state suggest that email is not easy work. It appears to require that people be focused when doing email and its use is also associated with being in a negative mood and with stress.

## 6.7    SUMMARY AND DISCUSSION: EMAIL AND MULTITASKING

Despite the advantages that email affords for the workplace, studies of email use reveal consistently that it is associated with interrupting work, a negative mood, a feeling of being overloaded, a loss of control and stress. I will now summarize and discuss more fully how email contributes to fragmenting work, through multiple ways: the sheer volume and continual incoming flow of email, the mental effort of reading, answering, and composing emails, the wide affordances of email which has affected the need for task management as well as how it represents work to information workers, and the social norms that have evolved around email. These reasons in fact may interact in ways that intensify the adverse effects of email.

### 6.7.1    THE CONTINUAL FLOW OF EMAIL

The continual flow of messages into the inbox highlights the sheer volume of email that people must manage. But the continual flow of email is just one part of the story to explain work fragmentation; users have an urge to continually check email. There are various proposed explanations for why people continually check their inboxes. Our informants described a feeling of being left out of the organization when their email was cut off. People may check to keep abreast of organizational events. Missing out on an important email from a project team or one's manager could have dire consequences. Innate curiosity about what messages have arrived (or whether any message has arrived) could also explain why people continually check their inboxes. Checking can also be due to habit. Self-regulation is theorized to follow a resource depletion model. When people expend resources to self-regulate in one type of behavior, it utilizes cognitive resources, leaving less resources available for other types of self-regulatory behaviors (Vohs and Heatherton, 2000). This finding suggests that if people were to intentionally limit their email checking, the resources expended for this effort could adversely affect their self-regulation in other workplace behaviors. Following this idea, perhaps it is easier to check one's inbox than to exert effort, or cognitive resources, for self-control to limit checking. Further research could be done to test this assertion.

What leads people to open emails as opposed to simply checking to see what is there? Managing emails potentially creates more work fragmentation. If one interrupts a task to open and respond to email, then it conceivably is harder to reorient back to the interrupted task. There is a greater cognitive shift and more time is invested in this activity compared to simply checking email. Innate curiosity about the contents of a message and the perceived relevance of the message for one's work can explain why people choose to read some messages over others (Wainer et al., 2011). This suggests that there are constant decisions being made when one checks their inbox: what the subject line conveys, who is the sender of the message, what utility might the message have, how much work will be involved in answering the message, and so on.

The asynchronous nature of email affords people the opportunity to answer emails later. However, it is not always the case of out of sight, out of mind: not all unanswered email is forgotten. Email is always lurking in the background. Important messages can be deferred (Dabbish and Kraut, 2006). This pending work could add to overload and stress as it is a reminder of the work that needs to be done.

### 6.7.2    THE EFFORT OF "DOING" EMAIL

Our studies reveal that reading and writing email messages require focused attention. One reason for the focused attention is that email is a pervasive medium. As a stored record, people need to be careful about what is written, as they are accountable for the written message. Often, some thought needs to be expended in composing messages. If more effort or cognitive resources are devoted to doing emails, then this could deplete people's resources for dealing with other work.

The effort of dealing with email is not just limited to the actual time that people answer and send emails. The work in "doing" email is also in its task management. Bellotti et al. (2005) identified challenges in managing email ranging from flagging important messages to keeping track of email threads and deadlines. They also found that people spend about 20% of their time simply organizing content. These activities are generally done as email is continually managed over the course of the day, and contribute to fragmenting work.

### 6.7.3    SOCIAL NORMS ASSOCIATED WITH EMAIL

Our interviews identified a social norm that has developed in the workplace: email must be responded to quickly. It is interesting that with email, an asynchronous communication medium, a social norm has developed of fast response associated with it that pushes it closer to being a synchronous communication medium. The participant described earlier in the chapter who kept a later schedule than her colleagues reflected this concern. Barley et al. (2011), in his study of email use, described a similar social norm where participants felt that they needed to respond to email quickly. The social norm of feeling pressure to respond to emails could lead people to self-interrupt to check if an important email has arrived and even to take actions to reinforce the norm. The expectation for fast response to email leads many people to keep their email client open on the computer interface so that they can be alerted as soon as an email arrives (or at least to check what arrives). When notifications are turned on, and when people are on high alert for incoming emails, then it is a recipe for self-interruption.

### 6.7.4    EMAIL AS A REPRESENTATION OF WORKING SPHERES

Email, which has expanded in its uses to become a far more comprehensive tool in the workplace than a communication medium, consequently encompasses more work. Barley (2011) suggested that it may not be email per se that creates a feeling of overload but rather the work that email creates. It is easier to delegate work through email in written form than in face-to-face interaction. It is also relatively easy to ask for information through email rather than looking up the information oneself. Email use thus not only creates work, but also represents work.

People switch between email and other work, often self-interrupting to do email. When work is interrupted, it requires more effort to reorient back into a working sphere. The results of the email cut off study show that without email, people switched computer screens (and at a courser level, they switched working spheres) less frequently when email was not available. One might ask whether it was to be expected that removing email would lead people to switch activities less frequently and focus a longer duration of time on other tasks. However, I argue that it is just as possible that email could have been removed from the workplace and people could have still switched tasks just as rapidly. In other words, there is some quality about email that leads people to switch tasks more rapidly.

Email can be viewed as managing work in working spheres. As I have highlighted, email has become far more than a communication medium. In all its various capacities of coordination, information seeking, task management, and archiving, email has become an interface to working spheres. When people deal with all aspects of email (checking, reading, answering, composing, deferring, filing) they are conducting work in various working spheres. Thus, dealing with different emails can also be regarded as switching between different working spheres. This raises an hypothesis as to why email is so distressing. Other communication mediums such as telephone or even face-to-face meetings may deal with working spheres in a more methodical manner than email. An example is that of meetings, which have agendas, usually planned and distributed in advance. They may cover several working spheres but each is allotted a set amount of time in a methodical manner.

Email on the other hand, is a conduit for information concerning multiple working spheres. Dealing with these multiple working spheres is generally done in a haphazard manner. Our attention constantly shifts as we address different tasks from different working spheres, sent through email. Managing emails, as entrants into working spheres, are anything but methodical. One might answer an email concerning the alpha project, while emails arrive concerning the beta and gamma projects. Shifting attention to attend to different working spheres brought up by emails, along with applying focused thought, could certainly contribute to stress.

The findings of email studies altogether suggest that email contributes to fragmenting work. In the next chapter we will explore in more detail how multitasking affects attention focus.

# CHAPTER 7

# Focus

Up until now, I have discussed the extent to which people are distracted while working with digital media. They continually switch among working spheres throughout the workday. But what leads information workers to be focused in the workplace? David Brooks, the op-ed columnist for the *New York Times*, in his column "The Art of Focus" describes that he is losing "the attention war" (Brooks, 2014). Are we really? How does multitasking affect information focus? This chapter examines the converse perspective of distraction and interruptions: characteristics of focus for information workers.

## 7.1 CONCEPTS OF ATTENTION FOCUS

There are several theoretical concepts that have been used to describe when people focus their attention on an activity. Absorption has been proposed as a personality trait that can predispose people to become deeply consumed by an activity (Telligen and Atkinson, 1974). Personality traits tend to be stable characteristics. However, absorption has also been considered as a transitory state, called cognitive absorption, which refers to when people experience total immersion in an activity, characterized by deep enjoyment, not being aware of the passing of time, a feeling of control, and curiosity. Cognitive absorption has been applied to understand technology adoption: it has been shown to be associated with ease of use and perceived usefulness of IT (Agarwal and Karahanna, 2000). A construct similar to absorption is cognitive engagement, also involving curiosity, deep interest and attention focus. However, it differs from absorption in that when people are cognitively engaged, they do not feel a sense of being in control of the situation (Webster and Ho, 1997).

More recently, the concept of mindfulness has been discussed frequently, often in the popular media. Classes in teaching mindfulness have begun to spread across companies in Silicon Valley (Schachtman, 2013). Mindfulness refers to a psychological state focused on phenomena (both externally and internally) with the emphasis that attention is geared to the present moment (Dane, 2011). Levy and colleagues (Levy et al., 2012) did an interesting experiment where they trained people in mindfulness meditation for eight weeks, and compared their performance in a simulated work environment with people trained in body relaxation, and a control group. The researchers found that with mindfulness training, participants spent a longer time on task with fewer switches between activities. These results suggest that it is possible to train people to become more focused in work. In organizational work, mindfulness has been considered an asset as it enables people to more skillfully respond to unexpected events (Weick and Sutcliffe, 2006).

A related concept is that of flow. Csikszentmihalyi (1990) has been a pioneer in studying the experience of flow, a state of total immersion in an activity. When people experience a flow state, they lose track of time, lose consciousness of the self, and feel in control of their environment. Flow is the deepest level of engagement in an activity of the concepts discussed so far. When in flow, the deep involvement in an activity can lead to creative thought. Artists, musicians, writers, dancers, and athletes have often reported being in a flow state. Yet people of all professions can also experience flow, from scientists to welders. When in flow, it is found that people feel highly challenged and make optimal utilization of their skills. Tasks that are not challenging rarely are associated with flow, whereas tasks that present challenges, that utilize one's skills, and that engage attention, can be associated with a flow experience (Massimini and Carli, 1998). Flow involves a balance of challenge and skill.

An aspect that these concepts describing attention share (cognitive absorption, cognitive engagement, mindfulness, flow) is that they explain times when people are deeply engaged in what they are doing. They also share the notion that these are satisfying, even gratifying experiences. They refer to transient states that people may experience depending on various conditions (both internal and external). They describe an active state of attention, what Weick and Sutcliffe (2006) described as: "*the capacity to take action.*"

Some psychological theories suggest that working memory may play a role in focused attention. Working memory performance appears to be related to the ability to control attention. It may not be the working memory storage per se that leads to a higher focus. Instead, it may be individuals' ability to filter out or suppress information that is irrelevant (Hester and Garavan, 2005). Studies show that increasing the load on working memory impairs people's ability to suppress irrelevant information (Roberts et al., 1994).

When people switch activities rapidly in the workplace, and when they are interrupted, either internally or externally, it takes them away from entering a state of deep engagement in any singular task. It is possible, however, that extreme multitasking, or switching rapidly among different activities, could in fact for some people possibly lead to a flow experience. We might expect that this could occur if such people also experience properties associated with flow while multitasking: a balance of being challenged and utilizing skills, losing self-conciousness, not being aware of time, and feeling in control of the situation. This might be expected of polychronic types, i.e., people who seek out and thrive from multitasking.

## 7.2    A THEORETICAL FRAMEWORK OF ATTENTION FOCUS

The studies of attention discussed (absorption, cognitive engagement, mindfulness, flow) have so far not examined *in situ* digital activity. But what happens in the actual workplace? When people are involved in work, what is associated with people's engagement in their digital activity? Are people focused when they manage their email or is this more of a mechanical task? What about Facebook use? Are people focused or rather bored when they do Facebook? Are there regular patterns that we can detect, of certain times of the day or of the week when people are more focused in their work?

In considering how to measure a focused state, it is useful to consider that there are different ways that people can be engaged in an activity. Simply measuring a single dimension of engagement does not reveal a full picture about how one relates to an activity. One can be engaged in work that is quite effortless, such as copying figures, or filling out forms. Playing solitaire is a good example of being engaged in an activity that is not challenging. On the other hand, one might be engaged in a task that is more consuming; it can be challenging and utilize one's skills. For example, in academia, it can be quite challenging to analyze data and write the results into an article. It may not be as challenging to format the article yet it still requires attention. It is important to consider both dimensions together in a measure of attention, as being both highly engaged and challenged in work is correlated with motivation, activation, concentration, creativity, and satisfaction (Lefevre, 1988). If we want to ultimately understand what leads people to be creative in the workplace, then it is more useful to measure how much attention is devoted to the activity along with how challenging is that activity.

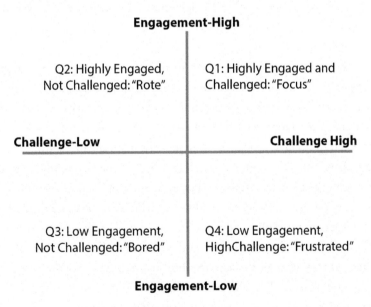

Figure 7.1: A theoretical framework of quadrants representing different attentional states in the workplace.

Challenge then refers to the amount of mental effort that one must exert to perform an activity. Engagement refers to a state of mind where one feels absorbed and dedicated in work (Schaufelli et al., 2002). For a review on measuring engagement and challenge to study work and leisure, see Hektner et al. (2007) and Macey and Schneider, (2008).

Figure 7.1 shows the theoretical framework presented in Mark et al. (2014b) to indicate different attentional states that are defined using the dimensions of engagement and challenge. The upper-right quadrant (Q1) shows high engagement and high challenge, and represents "focus," an attentional state when people feel absorbed in an activity, and are expending some amount of mental effort in performing that activity (reading, analyzing data, giving a lecture, writing a paper, and so on). The upper-left quadrant (Q2) characterizes an attentional state where one is highly engaged in an activity and not challenged. Many activities in information work can involve such types of attentional state such as transcribing numbers or filling out forms. This characterizes what we might think of as rote or mechanical work. This attentional state is labeled as "Rote." The lower-left quadrant (Q3) refers to an attentional state when one feels neither engaged nor challenged in their work and is labeled as "Bored." We expect that when people are not engaged in an activity and do not use mental effort, it should be boring. The lower-right quadrant (Q4) describes an attentional state where one is challenged but is not engaged in an activity. An example of frustrated work is when one is trying to figure out how to fix a technical computer glitch (which often happens at an inopportune time).

The characterization of "focus" in the framework in Figure 7.1 can be thought of as a precondition to flow. Flow involves deep concentration, engagement, challenge, and use of one's skills in an activity. It is possible that with extended duration of focus, and with a challenge to one's skill set, one could experience flow. However, true flow seldom occurs. Rather focus as a precondition to flow should be expected to occur far more often in an information work setting.

People likely change their attentional states throughout the day, with the task, interactions, digital media use, cognitive resources, stress, and other contextual factors. For this reason, it is important to take continual measures of attentional states, which can be done through the use of experience sampling. Experience sampling involves the use of probes, which are brief pop-up surveys presented to participants on the desktop. In the studies described here, people were probed on how engaged and challenged they were in the activity they just did. Also, they were asked to rate their mood (valence) and arousal, using Russell's circumplex model of stress (Russell, 1980). Experience sampling has been used extensively in research to measure the flow experience (Hektner et al., 2007). Next, I will present some results showing how attentional states exhibit temporal patterns, and how they correlate with mood and digital media use.

## 7.3    PATTERNS OF ATTENTIONAL STATES

Attentional states follow course patterns in information work. Temporal patterns refer to how attention is distributed over time. Activity patterns refer to how attention is correlated with the use of certain digital media. The results reported here are based on a *in situ* study of information workers (Mark et al., 2014b). The computer activity of participants was logged, and attentional state and mood were self-reported by participants as described above, using the experience sampling method.

Figure 7.2, reported in Mark et al. (2014b), shows how attentional states of focus, rote, and bored change over the course of the day. There were only a handful of self-reports of being frustrated, and so these were excluded from the analysis. The temporal patterns shown in Figure 7.2 are averaged over all days and all participants, from 7 a.m.–9 p.m. The left axis refers to the average seconds that people spend in a particular application (e.g., email, Facebook, productivity apps).

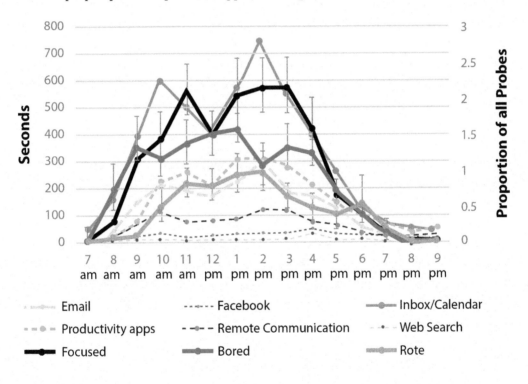

Figure 7.2: Temporal patterns of attentional states of focus, rote, and bored, throughout a typical workday.

There are some interesting patterns to the data. First, proportionally, information workers report being more focused than bored in the workplace. Second, people generally do not arrive at the office being highly focused. It takes time to ramp up focus, and for participants, on average, focus peaks in the morning at around 11 a.m. Then people break for lunch and their focus peaks again mid-afternoon, from 2–3 p.m. Boredom, on the other hand, peaks earlier in the morning, around 9 a.m., and then peaks again around 1 p.m. Rote work occurs most often (proportional to all attentional states) from around 11 a.m.–2 p.m.

Attentional states vary also with the digital activity that one does. Checking the inbox and calendar (not reading or writing emails) corresponds very closely to reports of being focused (see Figure 7.2). The use of what are known as productivity apps (e.g., Word, Excel, Power Point, Visual studio) follow loosely a similar pattern of how focused attention is distributed over the day. Remote communication such as video conferencing or Internet telephony is higher from mid-morning through mid-afternoon. The use of Facebook, non-work email (i.e., web email), and information seeking (i.e., web search) is done continually throughout the day in a fairly uniform manner.

When assessing total digital media use, on average, people report being most focused when doing email. In contrast, surfing the Internet, and using the Inbox/Calendar are associated with a bored state. Facebook use is also associated with a bored and a rote attentional state. When people switch computer windows (a proxy for switching attention), this is mostly associated with being bored. This makes sense, as when people switch attention rapidly, it is conceivable that they are not spending a long enough time on any site to enter a focused state.

What is the effect of a mid-day lunch break? People spend significantly more time on Facebook and personal email after returning from lunch than before breaking for lunch. They also switch their attention from screen to screen significantly more at the beginning of the day than at the end of the day. These results, together with the temporal pattern results, support the idea that it takes time for people to transition to focusing on work at the beginning of the day or after a break.

When viewed over the week, except for Tuesdays, people report being slightly more focused than bored. On Fridays, people report being more focused than either bored or doing rote work. Perhaps on Fridays, people tend to catch up on the work that they did not have time for during the earlier part of the week. If we look at feelings of boredom over the week, people are most bored on Mondays, and if we look just at feelings of doing rote work, Thursday is the day when most rote, or mechanical and routine work is done.

## 7.4    ATTENTIONAL STATE AND MOOD

As discussed earlier, studies have shown that being in a focused state is associated with a positive mood. Flow, absorption, and cognitive engagement have all been found to be associated with high positive affect (Agarwal and Karahanna, 2000; Csikszentmihalyi, 1990). Cziksentmihalyi (1990) found that teenagers reported being much happier when they were in a state of flow than when not. On the other hand, states of boredom have been found to be associated with negative affect (Massimini and Carli, 1998). But Schallberger (1995) found that being challenged in work could lead to both high positive and negative affect. One explanation for what seems to be an ambiguous state is that when people are challenged, they become aroused, which could intensify the feeling of either positive or negative affect. In other words, if one tends towards feeling positive, then when aroused, the feeling would be stronger.

But what about being focused in the workplace? Are people happiest in the workplace when they are doing focused work, as opposed to doing rote work or boring work? Referring back to the framework described in Figure 7.1, would a focused state be associated with a positive mood? Or rather, because focus also encompasses challenge, would it be associated with negative affect?

We investigated this question in the same study of information workers *in situ* (Mark et al., 2014b). We found that contrary to the previous studies of focused attention, the study participants reported the highest positive affect when they were doing rote work: being highly engaged but not very challenged, and were the least happy when bored.

Why would people not be the happiest when doing focused work? The theoretical framework of focus shown in Figure 7.1 utilized two dimensions: engaged and challenged. Thus, the measure of focus and rote work differed in the dimension of challenge. Perhaps when people are focused, being challenged can cause stress, which can lead to a more negative affect.

To answer the question of whether stress might explain why people are not happiest when focused (compared to doing rote work), we looked deeper into the mood ratings of valence and arousal collected through experience sampling. Russell's circumplex model of affect has four dimensions: happy, stressed, calm, and bad mood (Posner et al., 2005; Russell, 1980). Stress is defined as high arousal and negative valence.

When people reported being bored, doing rote work, or being focused, how did their moods coincide? Table 7.1 shows the counts of all participants' self-reports of mood by their attentional state. There was a significant relationship between mood and attentional state. We can see in Table 7.1 that, given that people reported being focused, most people self-reported as also being happy (48.8% of the time). Yet when people felt that they did rote work, they reported being happier *more often* (59.7% of the time). When people reported being bored, they mostly reported being in a bad mood (47.8% of the time). But if we look at the distribution of attentional states when people reported being stressed (the column percentages), we see that most of the time when stressed, people also reported being focused in their work. These results suggest that perhaps the reason why focused attention was not the most highly correlated with being happy is because people are stressed. The explanation could be that the underlying dimension for focus encompasses challenge. Being challenged can be stressful. Easy, or rote work that is not challenging, is not stressful and could lead to a more positive affect among information workers.

Table 7.1: Counts of self-reports: Mood Type over the different quadrants. Row percentages are above column percentages in parentheses.

| | Mood Type | | | | |
| | Bad mood | Stress | Calm | Happy | Total |
|---|---|---|---|---|---|
| **Bored** | 194 (47.8%) (67.8%) | 55 (13.5%) (22.6%) | 110 (27.1%) (60.4%) | 47 (11.6%) (11.0%) | 406 (100%) |
| **Rote** | 21 9.7%) (7.3%) | 39 (18.1%) (16.0%) | 27 (12.5%) (14.8%) | 129 (59.7%) (30.1%) | 216 (100%) |
| **Focus** | 71 (13.7%) (24.8%) | 149 (28.8%) (61.3%) | 45 (8.7%) (24.7%) | 253 (48.8%) (59.0%) | 518 (100%) |
| Total | 286 | 243 | 182 | 429 | 1140 |

## 7.5    ATTENTIONAL STATE AND SUSCEPTIBILITY TO DISTRACTION

What is the relationship of attentional state and distraction? Studies of multitasking and interruptions assume that people are focused in their work and then become distracted. The lure of email or Facebook could pull one away from their focused attention. But what if the opposite is true: What if a person's attentional state at a particular time makes them *susceptible* to distractions? Is it possible that a particular attentional state, such as feeling bored or feeling that work is rote, is a precursor to using Facebook, checking email, or having a face-to-face interaction? From this perspective, a person may first become bored in their current task, which makes them more easily distracted. They may then turn to check Facebook or email.

We tested this proposition (Mark et al., 2015). We examined three common but distinct types of workplace communications as potential distractors: email, Facebook, and face-to-face interaction—each of these differing in their online or offline nature and in being social or work-related. The email that we examined was a corporate email account and thus involved primarily a work-related interaction, Facebook was primarily a social interaction, and face-to-face could be either. Our approach was to examine whether people's attentional states would make them susceptible to distractions for different types of communications: social or work related.

Using experience sampling, people reported how engaged and challenged they were when they were probed. Using the framework of Figure 7.1, we looked at the three attentional states of focus, rote, and boredom (there were only a few frustration reports). After people reported their attentional state we then looked at the duration that people spent in each of the three communication types in a 10-min window of time following the probe. We controlled for the type of communication before the probe to rule out the possibility that a person was just continuing the behavior they were doing before the experience sampling probe occurred.

Figure 7.3 shows the results. For Facebook, the results showed that when people reported being in a rote state, they spent significantly longer on Facebook, compared to when they reported being in a Focused state. What about behavior that involves checking Facebook? The results of checking Facebook are consistent with results of the duration of Facebook: following a reported rote state, people checked their Facebook accounts significantly more times in the subsequent 10-min window of time.

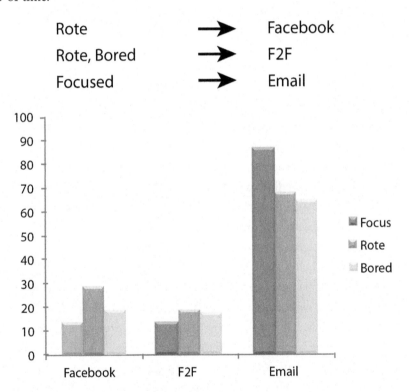

Figure 7.3: Attentional states prior to Faceboo, face-to-face interaction, and email use.

Face-to-face interaction was measured through the use of Sensecams, small wearable lightweight cameras that took continual photos about every 15 s. Face detection software was then applied to detect the presence or absence of a face in the photo. The results are similar to Facebook:

people were found to subsequently engage in more face-to-face interactions when feeling rote (engaged but not challenged) and least when they felt focused (engaged and challenged).

For email, participants were more likely to spend more time in email (in the 10-min window of time following the experience sampling probe) when they are feeling focused, compared to when they are feeling bored, or doing rote work.

The results thus show that when people are in a rote state (feeling engaged but not challenged), they subsequently spend more time on FB and check FB more, as well as having more F2F interaction. However, when people are in a focused state, they are more likely to then spend a longer time on email. Email use is also associated with arousal. Thus, when people are aroused and in a focused state, they then spend a longer period of time doing email.

## 7.6    SUMMARY AND DISCUSSION: FOCUSED ATTENTION IN THE WORKPLACE

A discussion of multitasking would not be complete without considering the converse perspective of interruptions and distractions: factors associated with focused attention. I began this chapter by presenting different constructs used in describing focus of attention. Of these, flow involves a balance of utilizing skills and being challenged, and people are deeply engaged in an activity. In this sense, the concept of focus I describe in our studies is most similar to a precondition of flow. We cannot say, however, based on our measure, whether people in our studies actually achieved a state of flow in the workplace. To measure flow, people need to keep a detailed diary describing the experience. This is a rich idea to pursue in future work studying attentional states of information workers.

Studies of flow (along with absorption, cognitive engagement, and mindfulness) reveal that when people are highly engaged in an activity, they feel positive. Yet, puzzlingly, we found that people were happiest when being engaged and not challenged, in other words, when doing rote and mechanical work. An explanation for the discrepancy of our results compared to the previous ones is that people actually were happy when experiencing both focused and rote work in our framework. They were simply happier, however, when doing rote work. Both focused and rote work involve a degree of engagement in an activity (see Figure 7.1). The dimension we defined as engagement is similar to the other constructs of absorption, cognitive engagement and mindfulness. However, these other constructs do not consider challenge as part of the definition. Flow, however, does include challenge. In other words, when the construct of attention is broken down according to whether one is challenged or not, then it reveals a difference in the degree of happiness experienced. A colleague of mine, a full professor of computer science in a top US university, after hearing this result of rote work told me that he recently derived satisfaction from spending time matching his socks after the laundry. He explained that he enjoyed doing it as he felt he was accomplishing something. Perhaps with rote work, people can feel short term gratification and a sense of accomplishment.

Different attentional states are associated with contextual factors in the workplace. People's attentional states shift as their online activities change: people are generally focused when doing email, while Facebook or face-to-face interaction more often does not require focused attention. There are also temporal patterns with attention focus. When people arrive at the office, in general, they do not "hit the ground running" by working in a focused state. Social and personal activities such as Facebook and personal email may help people to transition into a more focused pattern of work.

When we consider attention distribution over the course of the week, Mondays are the day when people are most bored. There has long been a debate on whether a "Blue Monday" effect exists (cf. Stone et al., 1985). This line of research suggests that people's mood is most negative on Monday. If so, it is possible that an explanation for the beginning of week negative mood is that people are actually bored on Mondays. As we found, boredom is highly correlated with a negative mood. Perhaps after a weekend break, it is hard for people to garner up resources to tackle interesting and challenging problems, at least initially. People are least bored on Fridays. This suggests a pattern where perhaps in the process of being involved in work over the course of the week, interest in work increases. There could, however, be a number of other underlying variables to explain this pattern, such as that people might choose to get more boring work out of the way early in the week, or that workplace demands lead them to work on different activities as the week progresses.

The large body of research on distractions and interruptions have not (pun intended) focused attention on what happens *before* a distraction. We found that the particular attentional state that people experience before a distraction makes people susceptible to certain types of distractions. If people are doing boring or rote work, they might be more easily distracted, and thus susceptible to doing a lightweight activity such as Facebook or having a face-to-face interaction. Email, on the other hand, occurs after people report having focused attention. People also report being more aroused when they do email. It could be that if people are already in a state of focus and high arousal, then they may feel "prepared" to attack email. If one has already garnered up their attentional resources, then it may be less effort to stay focused and continue to do an activity that requires focus. For lightweight distractions such as Facebook, it may not be the interruptions that break focus; it may be that lack of focus exists already, which makes people more prone to interruptions. If one is already doing rote work, why not continue to do another activity that does not involve challenge, such as checking Facebook?

Altogether, looking at attentional state and distraction suggests that people may continue to work in a manner that minimizes a transition of attentional resources. It may be less effortful to continue along at the same level of attention rather than switching to a more focused attentional state. An analogy is riding a bike. If one is riding along flat ground, it is more work to transition to ride up a hill. Usually we try to avoid riding up hills—if we spot a hill ahead, we may try to ride around the hill to remain on level ground. However, if one does attack that uphill climb and has started pedaling the bike uphill, and adjusted to a lower gear, then one is already in a routine for peddling fast with slow progress up the hill. If there is flat terrain ahead, and a new hill in sight, it may not be worth shifting the gears again for the level ground. On the other hand, if one is coasting downhill, it is easier to continue to coast rather than to pull the brakes to slow down, readjust gears, and then coast again. It is possible that focused attention may operate similarly. It may involve more cognitive resources to transition attentional states than to simply remain in the same attentional state, or rhythm, for a longer period of time. This could explain why, when people are already focused, they choose to do email and when people are already bored, they choose to do lightweight activities. Thus, it is important to consider attentional states as an explanation for why people switch activities and fragment work.

# CHAPTER 8

# Conclusions

In this book I discussed multitasking from various perspectives: activity switching, interruptions as triggers for activity switching, email as a major source of interruptions, and the converse of distractions: focused attention. All of these factors are components of information work. How can we make sense of these results to understand multitasking in the workplace, and the role of digital media?

Multitasking has become a way of life for information workers. As the empirical data presented in this book has shown, the work of information workers is characterized by their continual switching of attention throughout the day. Attention switching occurs whether it is viewed at a fine-grained level of events such as phone calls or email; it is also discernible when adopting a higher-level perspective of working spheres. Activity switching occurs irrespective of the nature of the communication, the artifacts or applications used, and whether it is online or offline activity. Information work involves multiple projects, multiple networks of people, and competing priorities that contribute to driving people to continually switch activity. Although most people are monochronic by nature, the current state of digital media in the workplace creates conditions that lead information workers to perform polychronic work.

In this book working spheres was introduced as a theoretical concept that can be used to understand multitasking. Our work shows that people organize and conceptualize their work in terms of cohesive units of work—individual events that are thematically connected. Using the concept of working spheres is a useful lens for understanding the nature of multitasking. Although people are performing individual events, they are actually constructing them into a coherent framework of a working sphere. Thus, when people are interrupted and when they resume work, they view such work fragmentation in terms of a higher-order notion—working spheres. When work is viewed at the granularity of events, people switch about every three minutes; when viewed at the granularity of working spheres, people switch on average every 10½ min. Regardless of how it is viewed, information work is highly fragmented.

For years, researchers have studied tasks in information work along a number of dimensions such as complexity, challenge, variety, engagement, information load, and whether collaborative or individual. A task dimension that has received little attention is the amount of fragmentation that is manifest in the course of performing the task. Fragmenting tasks disrupts the flow of attention and concentration and imposes an additional burden on the worker in performing the task. Further work can explore fragmentation as a function of the task itself. Here, relevant dimensions such as complexity, stimulation, challenge, and information load could play a role in affecting the amount of internal interruptions that one experiences with a particular task. Task dimensions could also influence the resumption of an interrupted task. Such work could lead towards developing a theory of self-interruptions.

There are a number of concerns about work being fragmented. First, multitasking imposes a cognitive burden. The work to manage activity switching requires cognitive resources above and beyond what is required to perform the work. When people are interrupted they have to maintain the states of different tasks. As the data in this book showed, people do not generally interrupt from a working sphere and then immediately return to it. Interruptions are typically nested; people work on average in two intervening working spheres before resuming an interrupted working sphere. Therefore, at any given time, people have multiple unfinished task states. There is a strain on working memory to keep track of these different task threads. Information work thus requires attentional resources not only to invest in the work itself but also to constantly switch and reorient among different types of activities, applications, and devices.

Second, multitasking as a common characteristic of information work has psychological implications. Interruptions were found to lead to stress based on a laboratory study which enables us to assess causality. The fact that only after one hour stress was increased suggests that over the course of a day of experiencing interruptions, stress might be higher. We also found that when email use was cut off, stress was lowered. These results on stress are consistent with a common complaint that we heard throughout our studies: informants felt overwhelmed and burned out with multitasking. Workplace stress can have negative impacts on health (Ganster and Schaubroeck, 1991). Further, stress experienced in the workplace during the day can have carry-over affects affecting personal and home life (Danna and Griffin, 1999). Therefore, it is possible that environments where people experience interruptions and multitasking could have detrimental affects on health.

Third, fragmented attention can potentially affect innovation. To achieve a state of flow, characterized by deep immersion and creative thinking, requires extended attention devoted to an activity. Spending 10 ½ min at a stretch in a working sphere before switching to another is not enough time to develop deep focus. On the one hand, activity switching could lead to new ideas through exposure to new information. On the other hand, continual switching interrupts the train and development of thought and prevents people from experiencing the conditions where flow can occur. Further, investing attention to maintain different states of work can detract from innovative thinking. Work fragmentation can inhibit innovation, as people need time and attentional resources to develop deep thought and creative solutions.

So why then, if multitasking requires additional cognitive resources, is associated with stress, and can hinder deep thought, do people switch their attention so rapidly in the workplace? Multiple factors contribute to encourage multitasking in the digitally enabled workplace. First, consider that even with the abundance of digital information available it is possible to still maintain a long period of focus on a working sphere, while putting other information out of mind. The abundance of information alone therefore is not a sufficient reason for multitasking. People can do mono-chronic work even in information rich environments. Yet our data show that they generally do not. In this book I presented other factors that, in addition to information abundance, could lead people to switch tasks. Information workers are involved in multiple working spheres (12 on average). The higher the number of working spheres, the more people there are in one's workplace network, and the more opportunities there are for interruptions by others. People are continually experiencing cues and interruptions in the workplace that influence them to switch working spheres. Digital information is also easy and fast to access, enabled by the computer interface where access points to information are always in the field of view. Further, the hypermedia structure encourages multi-tasking as the organization of information is mapped intuitively to how people reason.

A person's current attentional state may be another reason to explain multitasking. Our research suggests that particular attentional states are associated with different activities. If people are doing boring or rote work, they appear to be susceptible to being more easily distracted, and this could explain why people switch to do a lightweight activity such as Facebook or engaging in a face-to-face interaction. It may thus not be the interruptions that distract people; it may be that lack of focus exists as a precursor state that makes people more prone to distractions. In the digital workplace, if people are bored, it is far too easy to be lured into distractions, as a wealth of potential distractions are at our fingertips.

One trigger for multitasking is self-interruption. Perhaps one of the most intriguing find-ings is that people self-interrupt almost as much as they are interrupted by external influences. An interesting area for future research is to understand the reasons that lead information workers to interrupt themselves so frequently. The mechanism of self-interruptions still remains a black box. Dabbish et al. (2011) uncovered a set of factors influencing self-interruption; however a large por-tion of variance in self-interruption behavior still remains unexplained. More research is needed to consider additional causes such as task characteristics and individual traits to better understand the phenomenon in context.

Habit could be one reason for self-interruption. One mechanism for developing habits is through reinforcement. A powerful form of learning is through random reinforcement, or a variable interval schedule. If people receive rewards through email, Facebook, or other social media on a random basis (such as receiving an email from a long-lost friend) then this schedule is sufficient to reinforce the checking behavior of that application. However, randomly reinforced behavior is difficult to extinguish. If people received rewards regularly, for example with email and then the rewards suddenly stopped, then people would figure out rather quickly that rewards will no longer be coming. But if rewards are presented randomly, then it takes longer for people to figure out that the rewards have stopped. Although rewards with email may be few and far between, they gener-ally do keep coming. Randomly reinforced behavior is like playing the slot machines in Las Vegas. People keep playing the machines because they believe at some point that the reward will come.

Social norms can also explain why people self-interrupt, for example to check email or social media. Social norms are varied, ranging from the pressure to respond fast to colleagues, to feeling a need to keep up with news or social information. Our informants described that when they were cut off from email they felt they were missing out on information, despite the fact that they could speak with their colleagues face-to-face. Social norms in the workplace can be powerful reinforcers.

People could self-interrupt and switch activities to replenish their cognitive resources. However, this may be true if people are working extended periods on an activity and if they feel a need to take a break. But this seems to be an unlikely explanation if people are switching working spheres every 10 ½ min, and events much quicker, as our data show. Returning to the analogy of riding a bike, multitasking is like adjusting gears on a bike. If one is already focused on a task, then cognitive resources are invested in thinking deeply about that task, or solving a problem concerning that task. But when people switch tasks, it involves cognitive effort, like switching gears on a bike. They are changing course and have to readjust to the new direction. When gear switching is too rapid, or rather when attention shifting is too rapid, then cognitive resources can be depleted and stress can result, as was found with interruptions and email use.

How can we mitigate the potentially negative effects of multitasking? While self-discipline to remain focused is an admirable trait, few can claim they master it. The fact that people check email over 70 times a day suggests that such checking behavior could be habitual. Ingrained habits are hard to change (Wood and Neal, 2007). This suggests that some type of external support is needed to promote focus. A starting point could be to change email practices given the degree to which people interrupt to check and do email. The easiest solution is to close the email client. However, information workers in organizations are interdependent in a large web of interactions. It is difficult for any individual to not follow the social norms of email use. A single individual cannot simply pull the plug on email as participants did in our email cutoff study as they can be penalized by not getting access to information. Instead, solutions are needed at an organizational level on how to better manage email, which in turn will help with managing fragmented work. One method is for organizations to batch email at certain intervals, such as early morning, after lunch, and at the end of the workday. If people do not expect email to arrive for several hours then this could break their habit of continual checking. The amount of email could also be cut down through organizational practices such as referring organizational information to a pull-oriented channel instead of through email messages.

Other organizational solutions could be employed such as designating certain time periods as "no interrupt" zones. These, of course, would target external interruptions. However, given that research shows that external interruptions predict internal interruptions, it is possible that cutting down on external interruptions could break the overall pattern of interruptions. Some organizations are experimenting with flexible workspaces that can be configured into individual or collaborative spaces. A workspace designed to minimize distractions in the environment could promote focus.

The ad hoc strategies that information workers developed to manage their task switching (post-it notes, email reminders) point to the need to develop methodical support for multitasking. This points to technical solutions to help manage multitasking. There are a number of startups currently working to develop solutions to adapt email to a user's work patterns. Technical solutions can include monitoring a person's stress and mood with sensors. When a person's stress level exceeds a certain threshold then an intervention can be triggered, for example suggesting that the person take a break. An intervention could also be in the form of mindfulness cues as training in mindfulness shows promise in increasing focus (Levy et al., 2012) and could also have benefits in reducing stress. Other technical solutions can deploy sensors to monitor work patterns to determine opportune times to interrupt.

While digital media has offered us benefits that past generations could only dream of (in medicine, health care, education, transportation, communication, and other areas), it also poses challenges. Digital media has set the stage for multitasking. Again, we hear McLuhan's (1994) echo: the medium is transforming the structures that in turn give rise to new cultural practices. These cultural practices extend even to young children, as Eliza Dresang (1999) discovered. Mcluhan's earlier voice further resonates with us: *"Technology leads to new structures of feeling and thought."* Digital media is transforming structures of work, leading work, along with our attention, to become fragmented. Digital media has thus produced knock-on effects leading us to new arrangements in how we organize and perform work: it affects the nature of interruptions, how we switch between different activities, and even how we focus. The extent to which our very ability to focus is affected by digital media is something to contemplate. Digital media is here to stay, as is multitasking. The challenge in our current digital age is to learn how to adapt to the new structures we have created for ourselves.

# References

Acharya, U.R., Joseph, K.P., Kannathal, N., Lim, C.M., and Suri, J.S. (2006). Heart rate variability: A review. *Medical & Biological Engineering & Computing* 44, 12, 1031–1051. DOI: 10.1007/s11517-006-0119-0. 58

Adamczyk P.D. and Bailey B.P. (2004). If not now, when? The effects of interruption at different moments within task execution. *Proceedings of CHI'04*, 271–278. DOI: 10.1145/985692.985727. 33, 46

Agarwal, R. and Karahanna, E. (2000). Time flies when you're having fun: Cognitive absorption and beliefs about information technology usage. *MIS Quaterly*, 24 (4). 665–694. DOI: 10.2307/3250951. 67, 72

Altmann, E.M. and Trafton, J.G. (2002). Memory for goals: An activation-based model. *Cognitive Science*, 26, 39–83. DOI: 10.1207/s15516709cog2601_2. 36

Bailey, B. and Iqbal, S. (2008). Understanding changes in mental workload during execution of goal-directed tasks and its application for interruption management. *ACM Transactions on Computer-Human Interaction (TOCHI)*, 14 (4), 1–28. DOI: 10.1145/1314683.1314689. 33

Barley, S., Myerson, D., and Grodel, S. (2011). E-mail as a source and symbol of stress. *Organization Science* 22, 4 887–906. DOI: 10.1287/orsc.1100.0573. 53, 55, 64

Bellotti, V., Ducheneaut, N., Howard, M., Smith, I., and Grinter, R.E. (2005). Quality versus quantity: E-mail-centric task management and its relation with overload. *Human-Computer Interaction* 20, 1, 89–138. DOI: 10.1207/s15327051hci2001&2_4. 54, 55, 57, 64

Belloti, V., Ducheneaut, N., Howard, M., and Smith, I. (2003). Taking email to task: The design and evaluation of a task management centered email tool. *Proceedings of CHI 2003*, ACM Press, 345–352. DOI: 10.1145/642671.642672. 56

Benbunan-Fich, R., Adler, R., and Mavlanova, T. (2011). Measuring multitasking behavior with activity-based metrics. *ACM Transactions on Computer-Human Interaction (TOCHI)* 18.2 (2011): 7. DOI: 10.1145/1970378.1970381. 22

Blair, A. (2003). Reading strategies for coping with information overload, ca.1550-1700. *Journal of the History of Ideas*, 64, no. 1: 11–28. DOI: 10.1353/jhi.2003.0014. 1

Bluedorn, A.C., Kaufman, C.F., and Lane, P.M. (1992). How many things do you like to do at once? An introduction to monochronic and polychronic time. *Academy of Management Executives*, 6, 4, 17–26. DOI: 10.5465/AME.1992.4274453. 7, 49

Bluedorn, A.C., Kalliath, T.J., Strube, M.J., and Martin, G.D. (1999). Polychronicity and the Inventory of Polychronic Values (IPV): The development of an instrument to measure a fundamental dimension of organizational culture. *Journal of Managerial Psychology*, 14 (3/4), 205–230. DOI: 10.1108/02683949910263747. 7

Bohn, R.E. and Short, J.E. (2009). How Much Information? 2009 Report on American Consumers. Available http://hmi.ucsd.edu/pdf/HMI_2009_ConsumerReport_Dec9_2009.pdf. Accessed October 3, 2014. 2

Bolter, J.D. and Grusin, R. (2000). *Remediation: Understanding New Media*. Cambridge, MA: The MIT Press. 14

Borgman, C. (2000). *From Gutenberg to the Global Information Infrastructure: Access to Information in the Networked World*. Cambridge, MA: The MIT Press. 14

boyd, d. (2010). Social network sites as networked publics: Affordances, dynamics and implications. In Papacharissi, Z., Ed., *A Networked Self: Identity, Community, and Culture on Social Network Sites*. New York: Routledge, 39–58. 13

Brooks, D. (2014). The art of focus. opinion pages, *The New York Times*, June 2, 2014. 67

Brumby, D. P., Cox, A. L., Back, J., and Gould, S. J. (2013). Recovering from an interruption: Investigating speed- accuracy trade-offs in task resumption behavior. *Journal of Experimental Psychology: Applied*, 19(2), 95. DOI: 10.1037/a0032696.

Buehner, M., Koenig, C., Pick, M., and Krumm, S. (2006). Working memory dimensions as differential predictors of the speed and error aspect of multitasking performance. *Human Performance*, 19(3), 253–275. DOI: 10.1207/s15327043hup1903_4. 8

Burton, R. (1621). The anatomy of melancholy. Published by the Ex-classics Project, 2009. Available www.exclassics.com/anatomy/anatomy1.pdf. 1

Bush, V. (1945). As we may think. *Atlantic Monthly*. July, 1945, 1–12. 15

Campbell, D. (1988). Task complexity: A review and analysis. *The Academy of Management Review*, 13(1), Jan. 1988, 40–52. DOI: 10.2307/258353. 21

Carrier, L., Cheeverb, N., Rosena, L., Beniteza, S., and Changa, J. (2009). Multitasking across generations: Multitasking choices and difficulty ratings in three generations of Americans. *Computers in Human Behavior* 25(2), 483–489. DOI: 10.1016/j.chb.2008.10.012. 5

Castells, M. (2003). *The Internet Galaxy: Reflections on the Internet, Business, and Society*. Oxford University Press. 14

Collopy, F. (1996). Biases in retrospective self-reports of time use: An empirical study of computer users. *Management Science*. 42, 758–767. DOI: 10.1287/mnsc.42.5.758. 56

Conte, J. M., Rizzuto, T. E., and Steiner, D. D. (1999). A construct-oriented analysis of individual-level polychronicity. *Journal of Managerial Psychology*, 14, 269–288. DOI: 10.1108/02683949910263837. 8

Csikszentmihalyi, M. (1990). *Flow: The Psychology of Optimal Experience*. Harper & Row, NY. 68, 72

Cutrell, E., Czerwinski, M., and Horvitz, E. (2001). Notification, disruption, and memory: Effects of messaging interruptions on memory and performance. In *Proc. INTERACT 2001*, IOS Press, 263–269. 33

Czerwinski, M., Horvitz, E., and Wilhite, S. (2004). A diary study of task switching and interruptions. *Proceedings of CHI 2004*, 175–182. DOI: 10.1145/985692.985715. 21, 27, 33, 46, 56, 57

Czerwinski, M., Cutrell, E., and Horvitz, E. (2000). Instant messaging: Effects of relevance and timing. *Proc. of HCI'00, British Computer Society*, 71–76. 46

Dabbish, L., Mark, G., and Gonzalez, V. (2011). Why do I keep interrupting myself?: Environment, habit and self-interruption. *Proceeding of the twenty-ninth annual SIGCHI conference on Human factors in computing systems (CHI 2011)*. ACM Press, Vancouver, B.C, 3127–3130. DOI: 10.1145/1978942.1979405. 40, 41, 42, 50, 81

Dabbish, L.A. and Kraut, R.E. (2006). Email overload at work: An analysis of factors associated with email strain. In *Proc. CSCW 2006*, ACM Press (2006), 431–440. DOI: 10.1145/1180875.1180941. 55, 56, 57, 63

Dabbish, L.A., Kraut, R.E., Fussell, S., and Kiesler, S. (2005). Understanding email usage: Predicting action on a message. *Proceedings of CHI 2005*. DOI: 10.1145/1054972.1055068. 54

Dane, E. (2011). Paying attention to mindfulness and its effect on task performance in the workplace. *Journal of Management*, 37 (4). 997–1018. DOI: 10.1177/0149206310367948. 67

Danna, K. and Griffin, R.W. (1999). Health and well-being in the workplace: A review and synthesis of the literature. *Journal of Management* 25.3 (1999): 357–384. DOI: 10.1177/014920639902500305. 80

Donaldson, S. and Grant-Vallone, E. (2002). Understanding self-report bias in organizational behavior research. *Journal of Business and Psychology*, 17 (2), 245–260. DOI: 10.1023/A:1019637632584. 55

Dresang, E.T. (1999). *Radical Change: Books for Youth in a Digital Age*. H.W. Wilson, New York. 16, 83

Ducheneut, N. and Watts, L. (2011). In search of coherence: A review of email research. *Human-Computer Interaction*, 20:1-2, 11–48. DOI: 10.1207/s15327051hci2001&2_2. 54

Farhoomand, A.F. and Drury, D.H. (2002). Managerial Information Overload. *Communications of the ACM*, 45(10), 127–131. DOI: 10.1145/570907.570909. 54

Fisher, D., Brush, A.J., Gleave, E., and Smith, M. (2006). Revisiting Whitaker and Sidner's "Email Overload" ten years later. *Proceedings of CSCW 2006*, 309–312. DOI: 10.1145/1180875.1180922. 56

Ganster, D.C. and Schaubroeck. J. (1991). Work stress and employee health. Journal of Management 17.2: 235–271. DOI: 10.1177/014920639101700202. 80

Gillie, T. and Broadbent D. (1989). What makes interruptions disruptive? A study of length, similarity and complexity. *Psychological Research*, 50, 243–250. DOI: 10.1007/BF00309260. 46, 47

Golder, S., Wilkinson, D., and Huberman, B. (2007). Rhythms of social interaction: Messaging within a massive online network. *Communities & Technologies*, 41–66. DOI: 10.1007/978-1-84628-905-7_3. 5

Gonzalez, V. and Mark, G. (2004). "Constant, constant, multi-tasking craziness": Managing multiple working spheres. *Proceedings of ACM CHI'04*, Vienna, Austria, April 26–29, 113-120. DOI: 10.1145/985692.985707. 12, 22, 23, 24, 25, 27, 28, 30, 33, 35, 36

Greist-Bousquet, S. and Schiffman, N. (1992). The effect of task interruption and closure on perceived duration. *Bulletin of the Psychonomic Society*, 30(1), 9–11. DOI: 10.3758/BF03330382. 44

Hall, E.T. and Hall, M.R. (1990). *Understanding Cultural Differences*, Intercultural Press, Yarmouth, ME. 7

Hart, S. G. and Staveland, L. E. (1988). Development of a multi-dimensional workload rating scale: Results of empirical and theoretical research. In Hancock, P. A. and Meshkati, N., Eds., *Human Mental Workload*, Amsterdam, The Netherlands: Elsevier, 139–183. DOI: 10.1016/S0166-4115(08)62386-9. 47

Hektner, J., Schmidt, J., and Csikszentmihalyi, M. (2007). *Experience Sampling Method: Measuring the Quality of Everyday Life*. Sage, Thousand Oaks, CA. 70

Hester, R. and Garavan, H. (2005). Working memory and executive function: The influence of content and load on the control of attention. *Memory & Cognition*, 2005, 33(2), 221–233. DOI: 10.3758/BF03195311. 68

Hewlett, S.A. and Luce, C.B. (2006). Extreme jobs: The dangerous allure of the 70-hour workweek. *Harvard Business Review*, 84(12), 49–59, 162. 60

Horne, J.H. and Lupton, T. (1965). The work activities of 'middle' managers - An exploratory study. *The Journal of Management Studies*, 2, 14–33. DOI: 10.1111/j.1467-6486.1965.tb00563.x. 21, 32

Huang, E. and Lin, S. (2014). How does email use affect perceived control of time? *Information & Management*, 51, 679–687. DOI: 10.1016/j.im.2014.05.013. 54, 60

Hudson, J.M., Christensen, J., Kellogg, W.A., and Erickson, T. (2002). "I'd be overwhelmed, but it's just one more thing to do:" Availability and interruption in research management. *Proceedings of CHI 2002*, 97–104. DOI: 10.1145/503391.503394. 21, 34, 41, 46

Iqbal, S.T. and Horvitz, E. (2007). Disruption and recovery of computing tasks: Field study, analysis, and directions. *Proceedings of CHI 2007*, 677–686. DOI: 10.1145/1240624.1240730. 33

Iqbal, S.T. and Bailey, B. (2007). Understanding and developing models for detecting and differentiating breakpoints during interactive tasks. *Proceedings of CHI 2007*, pp. 697–706. DOI: 10.1145/1240624.1240732. 34

Jackson, T., Dawson, R., and Wilson, D. (2003). Reducing the effect of email interruptions on employees. *International J of Information Management*, 23, 1, 55–65. DOI: 10.1016/S0268-4012(02)00068-3. 56, 57

Jackson, M. (2002). *What's Happening to Home? Balancing Work, Life, and Refuge in the Information Age*. Notre Dame: Sorin. 22

Jing, J. and Dabbish, L. (2009). Self-interruption on the computer: A typology of discretionary task interleaving. In *Proc. CHI 2009*, ACM Press, 1799–1808. DOI: 10.1145/1518701.1518979. 36

Kahneman, D. (1973). *Attention and Effort*. Englewood Cliffs, NJ: Prentice-Hall. 8

Kieras, D., Meyer, D., and Ballas, J. (2000). Modern computational perspectives on executive mental processes and cognitive control: Where to from here. *Control of cognitive processes: Attention and performance XVIII* (2000), 681–712. 9

Klosterman, C. (2010). My zombie, myself: Why modern life feels rather undead. *The New York Times*, Dec. 3, 2010. 53

König, C.J., Oberacher, L. and Kleinmann, M. (2010). Personal and situational determinants of multitasking at work. *Journal of Personnel Psychology* 9.2: 99. DOI: 10.1027/1866-5888/a000008. 8

Kraut, R. E., Fish, R., et al., (1993). Informal communication in organizations: form, function, and technology. In Baecker, R., Ed. *Groupware and Computer-Supported Cooperative Work.* Morgan Kaufmann, 1993, 287–314. 39

Kushlev, K. and Dunn, E. (2015). Checking email less frequently reduces stress. *Computers in Human Behavior*, 43, 220–228. DOI: 10.1016/j.chb.2014.11.005. 55

Lefevre, J. (1988). Flow and the quality of experience during work and leisure. In Czikszentmihalyi, M. and Czikszentmihalyi, I., Eds. *Optimal Experience: Psychological Studies of Flow in Consciousness*, Cambridge University Press, Cambridge. 69

Leroy, S. (2002). Why is it so hard to do my work? The challenge of attention residue when switching between work tasks. *OBHDP*, 109, 3, 168–181. 36

Levy, D., Wobbrock, J., Kazniak, A., and Ostergren, M. (2012). The effects of mindfulness meditation training on multitasking in a high-stress information environment. *Proceedings of Graphics Interface 2012*, Toronto, Canada, 45–52. 67, 83

Macey, W. and Schneider, B. (2008). The meaning of employee engagement. *Industrial and Organizational Psychology*, 1. 3–30. DOI: 10.1111/j.1754-9434.2007.0002.x. 70

Mano, R. and Mesch, G. (2010). Email characteristics, work performance and distress. *Computers in Human Behavior*, 26, 61–69. DOI: 10.1016/j.chb.2009.08.005. 54, 55, 57

Mark, G., Iqbal, S., Czerwinski, M., and Johns, P. (2015). Focused, aroused, but so distractible: A temporal perspective on multitasking and communications. *Proceedings of CSCW 2015*, ACM Press. DOI: 10.1145/2675133.2675221. 12, 56, 62, 74

Mark, G., Iqbal, S., Czerwinski, M., and Johns, P. (2014a). Capturing the mood: Facebook and face-to-face encounters in the workplace. *Proceedings of CSCW'14*, Baltimore, MD, ACM Press. DOI: 10.1145/2531602.2531673. 62

Mark, G., Iqbal, S., Czerwinski, M., and Johns, P. (2014b). Bored Mondays and focused afternoons: The rhythm of attention and online activity in the workplace. *Proceeding of the thirty-second annual SIGCHI conference on Human factors in computing systems (CHI'14)*, ACM Press. DOI: 10.1145/2556288.2557204. 62, 70, 71, 73

Mark, G., Guy, I., Kremer-Davidson, S., and Jacovi, M. (2014c). Most liked, fewest friends: Patterns of enterprise social media use. *Proceedings of CSCW'14*, Baltimore, MD, ACM Press. DOI: 10.1145/2531602.2531662. 13

Mark, G. and Ganzach, Y. (2014d). Personality and Internet usage: A large-scale representative study of young adults. *Computers in Human Behavior*, 36, July 2014, 274–281. DOI: 10.1016/j.chb.2014.03.060. 51

Mark, G., Voida, S., and Cardello, A. (2012). A pace not dictated by Eelectrons: An empirical study of work without email. *Proceeding of the Thirtieth Annual SIGCHI Conference on Human Factors in Computing Systems (CHI'12)*, ACM Press, 555–564. DOI: 10.1145/2207676.2207754. 25, 57

Mark, G., Hausstein, D., and Kloecke, U. (2008). The cost of interrupted work: More speed, more stress. *Proceeding of the Twenty-Sixth Annual SIGCHI Conference on Human Factors in Computing Systems (CHI'08)*, Florence, Italy, ACM Press, pp. 107–110. DOI: 10.1145/1357054.1357072. 22, 42, 46, 47, 50

Mark, G., Gonzalez, V., and Harris, J. (2005). No Task Left Behind? Examining the Nature of Fragmented Work. *Proceedings of ACM CHI'05*, Portland, OR, April 2-7, 321-330. DOI: 10.1145/1054972.1055017. 23, 30, 32, 37, 40, 41, 46, 47

Mark, G. and Poltrock, S. (2004). Groupware adoption in a distributed organization: Transporting and transforming technology through social worlds. *Information and Organization*, 14(4), October 2004, pp. 297–32. DOI: 10.1016/j.infoandorg.2004.06.001. 27

Massimini, F. and Carli, M. (1998). The systematic assessment of flow in everyday experience. In Czikszentmihalyi, M. and Czikszentmihalyi, I., Eds. *Optimal Experience: Psychological Studies of Flow in Consciousness*, Cambridge University Press, Cambridge. 68, 72

Mazmanian, M., Orlikowski, W., and Yates, J. (2013). The autonomy paradox: The implications of mobile email devices for knowledge professionals. *Organization Science*, 24 (5). DOI: 10.1287/orsc.1120.0806. 17, 53

McCrae, R. and Costa, P. (1999). The five factor theory of personality. In *Handbook of Personality: Theory and Research*, Pervin, L.A. and Johns, O.P. New York: Guilford, pp. 139–153.

McLuhan, M. (1994). *Understanding Media: The Extensions of Man*. Cambridge, MA: The MIT Press. 3, 11, 83

Middleton, C. A. and Cukier, W. (2006). Is mobile email functional or dysfunctional? Two perspectives on mobile email usage. *European J. of Information Systems*, 15(3) 252–260. DOI: 10.1057/palgrave.ejis.3000614. 55

Milgrim, S. (1970). The experience of living in cities. *Science*, 167, March 13, 1970, 1461–1468. DOI: 10.1126/science.167.3924.1461. 12

Mintzberg, H. (1973). *The Nature of Managerial Work*. Englewood Cliffs NJ: Prentice Hall. 32

Mintzberg, H. (1970). Structured observation as a method to study managerial work. *The Journal of Management Studies*, 7, 87–104. DOI: 10.1111/j.1467-6486.1970.tb00484.x. 21, 23

Miyata, Y. and Norman, D.A. (1986). Psychological issues in support of multiple activities. In *User Centered System Design*, Norman, D.A. and Draper, S.W., Eds. Lawrence Erlbaum, Hillsdale, N.J., 265–284. 34

Mokhtari, K., Reichard, C. A., and Gardner, A. (2009). The impact of internet and television use on the reading habits and practices of college students. *Journal of Adolescent & Adult Literacy* 52(7), 609–619. DOI: 10.1598/JAAL.52.7.6. 5

Monsell, S. (2003). Task switching. *Trends in Cognitive Sciences*. 7(3), March 2003, 134–140. DOI: 10.1016/S1364-6613(03)00028-7. 9

Navon, D. and Gopher, D. (1979). On the economy of the human-processing system. *Psychological Review*, 86(3), May 1979, 214–255. DOI: 10.1037//0033-295X.86.3.214. 8

Norman, D.A. and Shallice, T. (1986). Attention to action: willed and automatic control of behaviour. In Davidson, R.J., Schwartz, G. and Shapiro, D, (eds)., *Consciousness and Self-Regulation*, 4, 1–18, Plenum Press. DOI: 10.1007/978-1-4757-0629-1_1. 8

Oberauer, K., Süß, H.-M., Schulze, R., Wilhelm, O., and Wittmann, W. W. (2000). Working memory capacity: Facets of a cognitive ability construct. *Personality and Individual Differences*, 29, 1017–1045. DOI: 10.1016/S0191-8869(99)00251-2. 8

O'Connail, B. and Frohlich, D. (1995). Timespace in the workplace: Dealing with interruptions. *Proc. Of CHI '95 Extended Abstracts*, 262–263. DOI: 10.1145/223355.223665. 34, 43

Olson, G.M. and Olson, J.S. (2000). Distance matters. *Human-Computer Interaction*, 15(2/3), 139–178. DOI: 10.1207/S15327051HCI1523_4. 39

Ophir, E., Nass, C., and Wagner, A.D. (2009). Cognitive control in media multitaskers. In *Proc. Natl. Acad. Sci. USA*, 106, 15583–15587. DOI: 10.1073/pnas.0903620106. 50

Pashler, H. (1994). "Dual-task interference in simple tasks: data and theory." *Psychological Bulletin.* 116(2), 220. 5

Perlow, L.A. (1999). The time famine: Toward a sociology of work time. Admin. *Science Quarterly*, 44, 57–81. DOI: 10.2307/2667031. 22, 34, 40

Posner, J., Russell, J.A., and Peterson, B.S. (2005). The circumplex model of affect: An integrative approach to affective neuroscience, cognitive development, and psychopathology. *Development and Psychopathology*, 17, 715–734. DOI: 10.1017/S0954579405050340. 73

Radicati, S. (2013). Email Statistics Report, 2013-2017, The Radicati Group. Available http://www.radicati.com/wp/wp-content/uploads/2013/04/Email-Statistics-Report-2013-2017-Executive-Summary.pdf. Accessed October 4, 2014. 16

Renaud, K., Ramsay, J., and Hair, M. (2006). "You've got e-mail!" … shall I deal with it now? Electronic mail from the recipient's perspective. *IJHCI* 21(3), 313–332. DOI: 10.1207/s15327590ijhc2103_3. 55, 56, 57

Roberts, R.J., Jr., Hager, L.D., and Heron, C. (1994). Prefrontal cognitive processes: Working memory and inhibition in the antisaccade task. *Journal of Experimental Psychology: General*, 123, 374–393. DOI: 10.1037/0096-3445.123.4.374. 68

Rouncefield, M., Hughes, J., Rodden, T., and Viller, S. (1994). Working with "constant interruption": CSCW and the small office. *Proc. CSCW'94*, 275–286. DOI: 10.1145/192844.193028. 33

Russell, J.A. (1980). A circumplex model of affect. *Journal of Personality and Soc Psychology*, 39, 1161–1178. DOI: 10.1037/h0077714. 70, 73

Ryan, T. and Xenos, S. (2011). Who uses Facebook? An investigation into the relationship of the Big Five, shyness, narcissism, loneliness, and Facebook usage. *Computers in Human Behavior*, 27, 1658–1664. DOI: 10.1016/j.chb.2011.02.004. 51

Sakitt, B. (1976). Iconic memory. *Psychological Review*, 83(4), July 1976, 257–276. DOI: 10.1037/0033-295X.83.4.257. 15

Salvucci, D.D. and Taatgen N.A. (2008). Threaded cognition: An integrated theory of concurrent multitasking. *Psychological Review*, 115(1), 101–130. DOI: 10.1037/0033-295X.115.1.101. 5, 9

Schachtman, N. (2013). Enlightenment engineers. *Wired*, June 18, 2013. 67

Schallberger, U. (1995). The influence of personality characteristics on self reports of working conditions. *Zeit. f. Experimentelle Psych*, 42(1). 111–131. 72

Schaufeli, W., Salanova, M., Gonzalez-Rom, V., and Bakker, A. (2002). The measurement of engagement and burnout: A two sample confirmatory factor analytic approach. *Journal of Happiness Studies*, 3, 71–92. DOI: 10.1023/A:1015630930326. 70

Schultze, U. and Vandenbosch, B. (1998). Information overload in a groupware environment: Now you see it, now you don't. *Journal of Organizational Computing and Electronic Commerce*, 8 (1998), pp. 127–148. DOI: 10.1207/s15327744joce0802_3. 54

Schwalbe, Kathy (2007). *Information Technology Project Management*. Boston: Course Technology Cengage Learning. 27

Schwartz, T. and Porath, C. (2014). Why you hate work. *The New York Times*, May 30, 2014. 4

Smith, M.L. (2010). *A Prehistory of Ordinary People*. Tucson: University of Arizona Press. 1

Sproull, L.S. (1984). The nature of managerial attention. *Advances in Information Processing in Organizations*, 1, 9–27. 21, 23, 24, 32

Stone, A.A., Hedges, S.M., Neale, J.M., and Satin, M.S. (1985). Prospective and crosssectional mood reports offer no evidence of a "Blue Monday" phenomenon. *Journal of Personality and Social Psychology*, 49, 129–134. DOI: 10.1037/0022-3514.49.1.129. 77

Su, N. and Mark, G. (2008). Communication chains and multitasking. *Proceeding of the Twenty-Sixth Annual SIGCHI Conference on Human Factors in Computing Systems (CHI'08)*, Florence, Italy, April 2008, ACM Press, 83–92. DOI: 10.1145/1357054.1357069. 25, 38

Szotek, A. (2010). "Dealing with my emails": Latent user needs in email management. *Computers in Human Behavior*, 27(2), 723–729. DOI: 10.1016/j.chb.2010.09.019. 55

Tellegen, A. and Atkinson, G. (1974). Openness to absorbing and self-altering experiences ("absorption"), a trait related to hypnotic susceptibility. *Journal of Abnormal Psychology*, 83(3), June 1974, 268–277. DOI: 10.1037/h0036681. 67

Turkle, S. (2010). *Alone Together*. Cambridge, MA: MIT Press. 53

Vohs, K. and Heatherton, T. (2000). Self-regulatory failure: A resource depletion approach. *Psychological Science*, 11(3), 249–254. DOI: 10.1111/1467-9280.00250. 63

Wacjman, J. and Rose, E. (2011). Constant connectivity: Rethinking interruptions at work. *Organization Studies* 32(7), 941–961. DOI: 10.1177/0170840611410829. 54, 56

Wainer, J., Dabbish, L., and Kraut, R. (2011). Should I open this Email?: Inbox level cues, curiosity, and attention to email, *Proceedings of CHI 2011*. DOI: 10.1145/1978942.1979456. 63

Webster, J. and Ho, H. (1997). Audience engagement in multi-media presentations. *Data Base for the Advancement in Information Systems*, 28(2), 63–77. DOI: 10.1145/264701.264706. 67

Weick, K. and Sutcliffe, K. (2006). Mindfulness and the quality of organizational attention. *Organizational Science*, 17, 514–524. DOI: 10.1287/orsc.1060.0196. 67, 68

Whittaker, S., Bellotti, V., and Gwizdka, J. (2006). Email in personal information management. *Communications of the ACM*, 49(1), January, 2006, 68–73. DOI: 10.1145/1107458.1107494. 54

Whittaker, S. and Sidner, C. (1996). Email overload: Exploring personal information management of email. In *Proc. CHI 1996*, ACM Press, 276–283. DOI: 10.1145/238386.238530. 54, 56

Wickens, C.D. (2008). Multiple resources and mental workload. *Human Factors: The Journal of the Human Factors and Ergonomics Society* 50(3), 449–455. DOI: 10.1518/001872008X288394. 6, 8

Wood, W. and Neal, D. T. (2007). A new look at habits and the habit-goal interface. *Psychological Review*, 114(4), 843. DOI: 10.1037/0033-295X.114.4.843. 82

Wu, A., DiMicco, J. M., and Millen, D. R. (2010). Detecting professional versus personal closeness using an enterprise social network site. *Proceedings of CHI'10*, NY: ACM Press, 1955–1964. DOI: 10.1145/1753326.1753622. 13

Yuzawa, H. and Mark, G. (2010). The Japanese garden: Task awareness for collaborative multi-tasking. *Proceedings of ACM Group'10*. Sanibel Island, Florida. ACM Press, pp. 253–262. DOI: 10.1145/1880071.1880114. 48

# Author Biography

**Gloria Mark** is a Professor in the Department of Informatics, University of California, Irvine. Her research focuses on studying the impact that digital technology has on people in real-world settings. She uses a range of sensors, biosensors, and other measures to conduct precision tracking of information workers' digital media use, focus, and mood. She received her Ph.D. in Psychology from Columbia University. She has worked at the German National Research Center for Information Technology (now Fraunhofer Institute) and has been a visiting researcher at Microsoft Research, IBM, Boeing, and The MIT Media Lab. In 2006 she received a Fulbright scholarship where she worked at the Humboldt University in Berlin, Germany. She has been the technical program chair for the premiere ACM CSCW'12, ACM CSCW'06, and ACM GROUP'05 conferences, has won and been nominated for best paper awards, and is on the editorial board of the top journals in the field of human-computer interaction: *ACM TOCHI* and *Human-Computer Interaction*. Her work has appeared in the popular press such as *The New York Times*, the *BBC*, *NPR*, *Time*, and *The Wall Street Journal*, and she was invited to speak at the South x Southwest (SXSW) conference.

CPSIA information can be obtained
at www.ICGtesting.com
Printed in the USA
LVOW02s1550111115

462080LV00002B/17/P

**DATE DUE**

| | | |
|---|---|---|
| | | |
| | | |
| | | |
| | | |
| | | |
| | | |
| | | |
| | | |
| | | |
| | | |
| | | |
| | | |
| | | |
| | | |
| | | |
| | | |
| | | |
| | | |